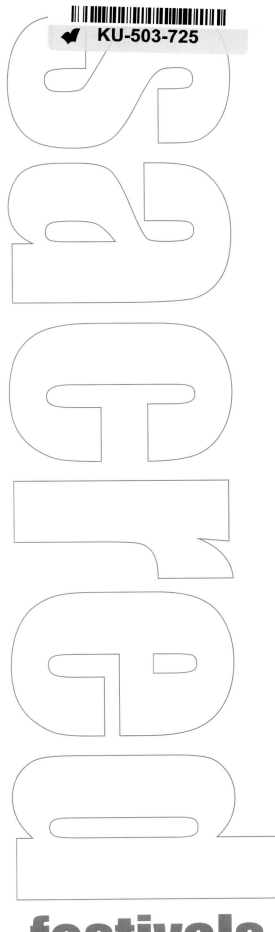

sacred

festivals

# sacred

## festivals

MQP
MQ Publications Ltd

291.36
HUN

# introduction

Somewhere in the world, on any given day of the year, there is a festival or pilgrimage. Some are celebrated against a backdrop of the world's most stunning landscapes; others release on to modern streets the atavistic beliefs and pulsating rhythms of an earlier age. And all the extraordinary rituals and fantastic imagery are created by the participants themselves, not by Disney or Hollywood.

Working as a television producer has given me access to hundreds of festivals around the world and over the last twenty-five years or so, learning about and witnessing these has become something of a passion. Experiencing them at close quarters is, in my view, the nearest we can get to travelling back through time. As a photographer I think of them as 'snapshots in time', where, on a very specific day, life and local customs can be viewed as they were hundreds, and in some cases, thousands of years ago. It is said, for instance, that the Kumbh Mela (see page 22) has been taking place for three thousand years. Indeed, were it not for the inconvenience of the camera not having been invented, many of the photographs here could have been taken centuries ago.

Even in the twenty-first century some countries seem to have festivals almost daily. I have a calendar of festivals in Bali numbering around two hundred – a month! Every weekend during the summer months is *fiesta* time in Spain and Portugal, and India is said to have more festivals than days in the year. These usually commemorate gods and goddesses, prophets, saints and religious gurus, but also honour trees, mountains and rivers, the coming of the monsoon or the beginning of spring. They are religious in origin, but they are also opportunities for social and cultural activities as well as providing a link between the home and the world outside. In today's ever more homogeneous world, even festivals with no deep spiritual roots help reinforce a village or town's past, giving the community a sense of identity and highlighting the way their ancestors lived, such as Çirit in Turkey (see page 94) or Praznik Cevera in Russia (see page 62).

Some of the festivals in this book are well known, but others are more obscure. Although their whereabouts do not always appear on the orthodox travel map, these 'time capsules' are readily accessible to the adventurous traveller, and some of them can be found surprisingly close by. For years I drove regularly through one of England's most industrialised areas, quite unaware until recently that I was passing close by the location of the strange and picturesque Abbots Bromley Horn Dance (see page 152).

Certain great religious festivals have spread around the globe, evolving to reflect local cultures. Carnival, for example, originated in France, where a fat ox was paraded through the streets of Paris on Shrove Tuesday, Mardi Gras, followed by a rowdy procession enabling the populace to let off steam before their forty days of fasting during Lent. Spectacular Carnival parades, lasting a fortnight or more, have become a colourful attraction throughout Catholic Central and South America, and New Orleans' Mardi Gras is world famous. In parts of Germany Shrove Tuesday is Fastnacht, and a *fastnachbar* is a boy dressed as a bear, who spends that day dancing with women – an ancient fertility rite! In Ireland, however, Carnival is a time for getting married, since weddings are banned during Lent.

It is astonishing that these cultural fragments of the past have managed to survive, virtually intact, into the present day. Inevitably, however, the shape and form of these festivals and pilgrimages will change and decline as the celebrants become rapidly acculturated. The Chinese recently announced that they were evaluating a proposal for an airport near Xiahe, in eastern Tibet. Xiahe is so small that it is hard to pinpoint it on even the most detailed of maps. It will be a major engineering challenge to construct an airport at an altitude of over 3000 metres, but if the project is rubber-stamped, it will have an immediate and detrimental cultural effect on the thousands of nomads living in the surrounding grasslands – and, of course, on the astonishing Grand Summons of the Labrang Monastery (see page 38). The world over, remote villages are being exposed to satellite television broadcasting, with an unavoidable impact on their lifestyles and expectations. Yet I've been aware of an increasing number of *young* celebrants participating in festivals where there are very strong spiritual links, and even though these devotees may wear designer trainers under their costumes, or queue for burgers between processions, their religious fervour is no less diminished. It is heartening to find tradition passed on from generation to generation, and – a note of optimism – I have found participants young and old, from Allahabad to Zacatecas, to have an unshakeable belief that the future will be better than today.

This book represents over a quarter of a century of amazing journeys and experiences, and I very much hope that it will inspire other intrepid travellers to step over the threshold of the twenty-first century and travel back through the centuries.

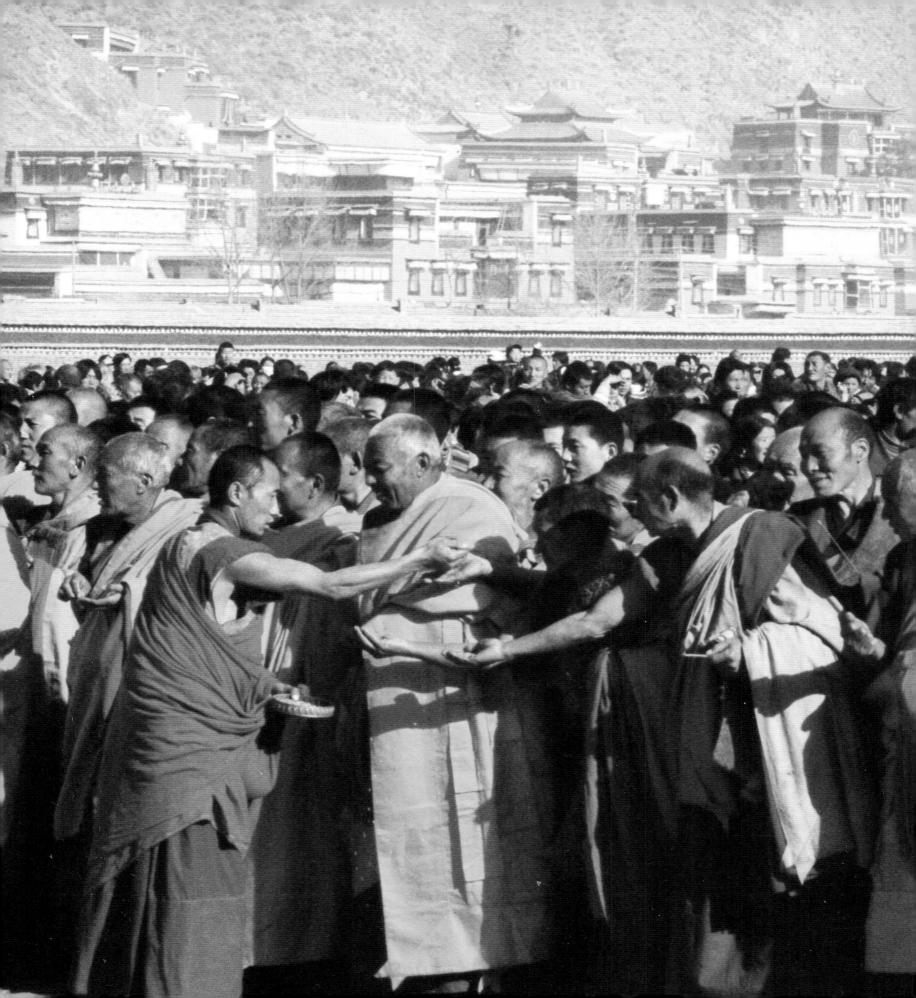

## pilgrim's rules

While browsing in a bookshop recently, I found a copy of *The Wanderings of Brother Felix Fabri in the Holy Land,* published in 1484, which included 'The Pilgrim's Rule'. As I began to read it, I realised how pertinent Brother Felix's observations were in relation to my own travels. He set out twenty-seven articles, or rules, to visiting spiritual places, and these are still just as appropriate today as they were over five hundred years ago. Here are some of the highlights:

**SECOND ARTICLE:** No pilgrim ought to wander alone about the holy places without a guide because this is dangerous and unsafe.

**FIFTH ARTICLE:** Let the pilgrims beware of chipping off fragments from the holy sepulchre, and from the building at other places, and spoiling the hewn stones because this is forbidden under pain of ex-communication.

**SIXTH ARTICLE:** Pilgrims must not deface walls by drawing their coats-of-arms thereon, or by writing their names.

**FIFTEENTH ARTICLE:** Let no pilgrim put upon his head white turbans, or wind white cloths or napkins about his head when there are Saracens present, because they consider themselves to be privileged to do this.

**EIGHTEENTH ARTICLE:** Let every pilgrim carefully guard his own property, and never leave it lying about in any place, otherwise it will straightaway vanish.

**TWENTY-THIRD ARTICLE:** Let the pilgrim especially beware of laughing to scorn those who are praying and practising the postures required by their faith.

**TWENTY-FIFTH ARTICLE:** Pilgrims must not grudge to pay money to save themselves from the many annoyances which beset them, but when money has to be paid they must give it straightaway without grumbling.

# devi gureşi, kuşadasi

Ipci, the camel of the man who sells rope, and undefeated champion of Asia Minor, was there; so were the camels of Yusuf the Cook and Khazim the Chauffeur, Black Paradise, The Rich One, The Aggressive One, Indefatigable, Happy, Fire and Fate, and The Pumpkin – 48 camels altogether, coming to fight for the Grand Championship of Kuşadasi.

Camel fighting is uniquely Turkish, for nowhere else do they fight professionally. It is thought that the Greeks first practised the sport several thousand years ago when owners of rival camel caravanserai wagered their finest animals. Fighting was introduced into western Turkey about a hundred years ago when Nasuf, son of Haci Mehmet, challenged Nazilli the Greek. Now, in the province of Aydin, contests take place every weekend during the rutting season of January and February when the snow is melting on the mountains and the days are cool.

In this remote area of Turkey, camels are normally used as beasts of burden, transporting the olive crop down into the towns. But fighting camels – haughty, vindictive and picked for their meanness – are never used as pack animals. They are a hybrid, called *tulu*, bred from a female Arabian camel with one hump and a male Bactrian (originally from the steppes of Russia) with two. Naturally aggressive, they start fighting at the age of five, are at their peak at fifteen, and live for about forty years. During the summer they are fed a special diet of wheat, barley and oats which enables them to build up their weight to a colossal 1200 kilos (a normal camel hits the scales at around 400 kilos).

At the end of November, as they prepare themselves for the breeding season, these great animals become exceedingly irritable. Their coats thicken, their hooves close up and their tails stand erect. They eat little, nourishing themselves from the fatty tissue in the hump, and froth at the mouth. They fight for the attention of a female, who is usually placed attentively nearby, and in a survival-of-the-fittest contest will fight to the death, the winner suffocating his challenger by knocking him down and lying on top of his head. But fights today are stopped before this happens, for a champion camel is worth at least 7 billion lire.

The contests at Kuşadasi take place over two days. The camels are paraded around the town, each animal saddled with a pack, gaily decked out with bells of varying sizes, rugs, embroidery, and blue beads to ward off the Evil Eye. Dancers and gypsy musicians playing drums and the ancient double-reeded shawm precede the procession, and the cacophony of sound stirs up the male camels to produce the required effect: they glare at each other, shift restlessly, and belch enormous quantities of foaming white spittle.

**page 14-15** Tulu camels, half Arabian and half Bactrian, are specially bred for the extraordinary wrestling championships which take place each spring and are unique to western Turkey.

**page 17** top An incongruous sight as an owner walks his animal through the noisy traffic of Kuşadasi on the way to the Grand Championship.

**page 17** bottom The camels only fight during the rutting season, and the owners encourage the natural aggression of their animals by keeping a female close by. The frothing white spittle is a sign of great agitation and irritability in the male.

**page 18** The bookmaker is sitting on a pile of Turkish carpets that winning owners can choose from, but substantial cash bets are also taken throughout the day.

**page 19** top and bottom Dancers and Gypsy musicians playing drums and the ancient double-reeded shawm create a cacophony of sound that apparently annoys the camels and increases their aggression even more.

**page 20** As a fierce fight reaches its climax, the camel on the right is in a winning position, and if the fight were allowed to continue he would suffocate his opponent by leaning on his head.

**page 21** The camels competing in the championships are kept muzzled until they are brought out to wrestle.

Ten thousand people paid to watch the Sunday contest. At stake were twenty-four Turkish carpets worth 130 million lire each, and a cash prize for the champion's owner of 240 million lire. The rules were somewhat incomprehensible. Five referees categorised each fight into *ayak* (foot), *orta* (middle), *basalti* (lower head), or *bas* (head), and animals were matched according to their style of fighting – 'the left hander', 'the camel who hooks the hooves of his rival', 'the one who crushes his opponent's head under his two front hooves'.

The bouts usually lasted about fifteen minutes, the winner being decided either when his opponent was half-suffocated, snorting in pain, or had been knocked down or, as frequently happened, was chased off into the crowd. The watching enthusiasts would then hoot, whistle, and cat-call as the musicians were brought on to stir up additional excitement for the next contestants. After seven hours of vicious excitement came the climax, when the Crazy One fought the Undefeated Camel of the Man Who Sells Rope – Ipci. Who won, of course.

During the night three thousand loudspeakers continuously blared out devotional songs interspersed with announcements relating to the thousands of people who had been reported lost around the *mela* ground. The cacophany created by the excited chatter of millions of pilgrims rose to a high-pitched wail as the auspicious *shahi snan*, the day of the royal bathing, dawned at exactly five-twenty in the morning. This was the day of Makar Sankranti when, according to the priests, the planets aligned into a formation not seen for 144 years, and in 2001 the greatest ever gathering of humanity was drawn to the confluence of the sacred rivers of the Ganges, the Yamuna and the mythical Saraswati.

Up to seventy million people are estimated to have attended the forty-two days of religious pilgrimage intertwined with carnival that is the Maha Kumbh Mela, the Great Festival of Elixir. *Kumbh* literally means 'pitcher' and the festival celebrates the triumphant recovery of the nectar of immortality which, during the churning of the oceans, had been poured into a heavenly *kumbh*. Demons, with their superior strength and strategy, stole the nectar, but after protracted combat with them Jayanta, the heir-apparent in heaven, wrested it back. His journey home took twelve celestial days, equating in Hindu mythology to twelve mortal years, and on the way four drops of nectar fell on Indian soil: at Haridwar in the state of Uttar Pradesh, Ujjain in Madhya Pradesh, Nasik, just southwest of Bombay, and Prayag on the outskirts of the city of Allahabad. Every three years for three thousand years a Kumbh Mela has been held at each location in turn, and Hindus believe that bathing at any of these holy places will cleanse and absolve them of all evil acts that they, and eighty-eight generations of their ancestors, have ever committed. In the significant twelfth year the great – *maha* – festival comes to Prayag (a Hindi word for 'confluence'), where the waters of India's sacred rivers meet: the holiest place in Hinduism.

The Kumbh today is not just about seeking salvation in the waters of the Ganges; it is also about the logistics of supporting this enormous congregation. In just two weeks, the 2001 festival site swelled from a few hundred tents on the dried-up pre-monsoon river bed into one of the largest cities on earth, accommodating a greater population than New York, Tokyo and London combined. In four months and on a desultory budget, the *mela* authorities constructed over 720 kilometres of streets, lit by 15,000 lights. They dug 19,000 trench latrines and employed 7000 street cleaners. They erected 50,000 telegraph poles, installed 16 hospitals and 28 police stations, and provided 50,000 litres of drinking water a day fed through 250 kilometres of piping. To provide the pilgrims with three free meals a day from the *akhara* (religious 'regiment') they supported, the organisers trucked in 13,000 tonnes of flour, 8000 tonnes of rice, 5000 tonnes of sugar and 11 million litres of kerosene to cook it on. Much of this food was paid for by wealthy donors; as one of them remarked to me: 'Peace comes with giving.'

Shortly after midnight on the day of Makar Sankranti, tens of thousands of devotees were already making their way across the narrow pontoon bridges that straddled the Yamuna River (some reports suggested they were crossing at the rate of 400,000 an hour) to reach the Sangam, the meeting point of the three rivers, to bathe on this most auspicious day. The *sadhus*, the holy men from the thirteen *akharas*, began their spectacular but noisy march about three hours later, the processions led by the spiritual leader, the *mahamandaleshwar* of each *akhara*, carried on a gilded palanquin or velvet-robed horse. Then, inching their way forward shoulder to shoulder towards the Ganges, came the naked dreadlocked *nagas*, feared for their magical powers. Wielding spears, swords and tridents that recall their warrior origins, they are covered only in ash from the dead.

These warrior-monks, many of whom had journeyed down from their Himalayan retreats for this Maha Kumbh Mela, take the ascetic life to extremes, renouncing all worldly pleasures and pursuits and consider their ash coating the only clothing they require. They say that punishing the body is the path to enlightenment; certainly after they had completed their sacred dawn bathing ritual they were all shaking violently from the exceptional chill.

This year, the *nagas* of the Nirvani *akhara* were the first to dash headlong into the icy water, but in previous years violent arguments have broken out between rival factions as to which group should bathe first. In 1953 a dispute resulted in a stampede of pilgrims being pushed into the Ganges and an estimated seventy thousand drowned in the (then) fast-moving current. In 1977 another dispute ended with twenty *nagas* being decapitated in the river.

The *sadhus* and *nagas* undoubtedly provided the colour and spectacle at this Kumbh Mela but the overriding impression for the visitor was the sanctity of the gathering. Secular music may have blared out from loudspeakers every few paces along the dusty streets, but in this vast tented city there were no shops or cafés, no street vendors, no ice cream or candy floss stalls, and no Coca-Cola machines. All vehicles were banned. For the millions who had journeyed through India, their worldly possessions carried on their heads, in order to bathe in the Ganges at this most propitious time, it was an act of faith and the experience of a lifetime. As one pilgrim expressed it: 'Bathing here brings internal peace. My sins will be cleansed from my past life as well as this one, and then I'll be pure for the next.'

**page 22-23** It is estimated that 100,000 pilgrims an hour bathed in the holy waters of the Sangam on Shahi Snan, the first of the Royal Bathing Days, which in 2001 fell on 14 January. By shortly after dawn the shoreline and shallows were teeming with devotees immersing themselves.

**page 25** Young boys, attired in the most opulent and lavish of ceremonial costumes, take on a temporary gender change during the course of the Kumbh, and are worshipped as living female goddesses. Their feet are not allowed to touch the ground and they are carried everywhere by their fathers or guardians.

**page 26-27** Just after dawn, the *nagas* of the Nirvani *akhara* wait to enter the sacred waters of the Ganges. Their ghostly appearance is achieved by coating their bodies with the ash of the dead.

**page 28-29** *Nagas* of the Juna *akhara* rush headlong into the Sangam. At each Kumbh Mela there is fierce competition among the *akharas* to be first into the waters.

**page 31** top The Maha Kumbh Mela lasts 42 days and many pilgrims spend part of each day bathing in the Sangam.

**page 31** bottom Devotees make their way at dawn on Makar Sankranti – on this day in 2001 the planets aligned into a formation not seen for 144 years.

A few years ago I was working on a television series on the French Foreign Legion. We had already filmed the induction of new recruits at the Legion headquarters in Aubagne, near Marseilles, and now wanted to follow their lives after basic training, when they were posted to overseas *départements* or former colonial territories. The liaison officer in Aubagne suggested that we film the arduous jungle-training programme they were operating in French Guiana. No one seemed to know very much about this small South American outpost of France, other than it was the home to one of the largest snakes in the world, the anaconda. Life there was so tough, it transpired, that legionnaires were paid an additional supplement merely to survive the rigours of the exceptionally unpleasant jungle environment. Until the 1950s the offshore Devil's Island was used as a penal colony to house France's most dangerous convicts; Henri Charrière, author of *Papillon*, was one of its most notorious prisoners. One of the Legion's roles was to protect the European Arianne Space Centre at Kourou, which had been carved out of the jungle by the Legion's engineers in the 1970s, and it was to Kourou that we went.

After a week filming in the rainforest, we took a much-needed short break to recover from the attacks of the vicious mosquitoes that were endemic there. Colonel Pau, commander of the 3ème Régiment Etranger d'Infanterie, recommended I drive down to the capital, Cayenne, about 160 kilometres along the coast. Mardi Gras was about to start, he reminded me, and said the celebrations in Cayenne had a reputation for truly spectacular costumes and imagery.

Mardi Gras is marked in exuberant fashion all over the Christian world. Traditionally, this was the last day before the fasting of Lent began. Foods such as meat, butter and eggs would then be forbidden, so stocks had to be eaten up by the day before, a wonderful excuse for a huge feast on Mardi Gras – Fat Tuesday. I had previously witnessed Mardi Gras festivities in Trinidad and Tobago, and this lesser known festival, in the town that gave its name to a red hot pepper, was no less noisy, colourful and exciting.

Mardi Gras in Cayenne is principally a Creole event, with musical and drumming participation from the town's Brazilian and Haitian communities. As in most other Latin American countries, the costumes here are very elaborate, and the dancers spend a considerable percentage of their annual wages on them. On the Monday, Lundi Gras, the institution of marriage is ridiculed with mock wedding parties and role reversals, building up to the final frenzy of Mardi Gras itself. Some of the women disguise themselves as Touloulous and, in a dance known as Chez Nana, Au Soleil Levant, ask the men to dance – the men mustn't refuse! Vaval, representing the devil and the soul of Carnival, appears among other dancers who wear red costumes with horns of fruit. Later that night, Vaval (in the form of a straw doll) is burnt, and the mourners in the final parade turn out strikingly dressed all in black and white.

page 32-33  Although most of the costumes are influenced by European festive style, particularly that of the Carnival of Venice, the majority of the celebrants at Cayenne's Mardi Gras are Amerindian.

page 35  The cornucopia of fruit on this dancer's head represents Vaval, the soul of Carnival.

page 36-37  Despite its religious origins, the enduring image of Mardi Gras is of outrageous costumes, flamboyant dancing and naked flesh.

# grand summons

We were met at Lanzhou's bleak airstrip in the arid, mountainous region of Gansu by our interpreter, Steed. 'Are you named after John Steed, star of *The Avengers*?' I asked. How else could he have acquired this archetypically English name while living in a remote Chinese province bordering Tibet? But he looked blankly at me, and I subsequently discovered that he was named after a horse!

Lanzhou, once a strategic base on the ancient Silk Road, was the starting point for a journey to remote Xiahe for the Grand Summons Ceremony of the First Moon at the Labrang Monastery, which effectively heralds the start of the Tibetan New Year. I'd found Lanzhou featured on a WHO internet site as it has the dubious claim of being the world's most polluted city, due to the size of its petrochemical industries. Nestling in a steep-sided, windless valley known as the Gansu Corridor and surrounded by the Qilian mountains, the pollution over the city sits as a thick grey cloud through which the sun barely penetrates. The gloom is compounded by the fact that the whole vastness of China adheres to Beijing time, and so the winter dawn does not reach Lanzhou, some 1800 kilometres west of Beijing, until about ten o'clock in the morning.

Xiahe is a day's drive from Lanzhou. Three hours of travelling through a landscape of brown dust without a visible blade of grass or vegetation brought us to the Muslim town of Linxia, where we stopped to buy a Tibetan horse rug. The market stalls here were piled high with animal skins, particularly leopard. Driving on, always upwards, brought us at last to Xiahe. We were now at around 3000 metres and the change in the environment was dramatic: another vast, dry valley set among even higher mountains, but here the sky was a brilliant azure.

Xiahe, in a region known as Eastern Tibet, is considered to be the leading Tibetan monastery town outside Lhasa and is the centre for the Yellow Hat sect of Tibetan Buddhism. The eighteenth-century Labrang Monastery today houses about 1600 monks, a significant reduction from the four thousand that lived here prior to the Cultural Revolution. The most revered figure here, as in other Tibetan Buddhist monasteries, is The Living Buddha.

I had first travelled through China as a television reporter in the 1970s, immediately after the Cultural Revolution, and on subsequent assignments felt that western acculturation was rapidly reaching the furthermost parts of the country. But not here. The thousands of nomads from the grasslands who were pouring into Xiahe in readiness for the Grand Summons created a picture of a world suspended in time, exotic figures in fur hats, leather boots and flowing, ankle-length robes with immensely long sleeves that hid their hands. Both men and women sported necklaces of red coral beads and, draped shawl-like over their shoulders, leopard skins. (These could be purchased from most of the stalls set up along the main street, but stall-holders were obviously aware they were illegally selling pelts of endangered species, because they would immediately throw a blanket over the skins when I attempted to photograph them.)

page 38-39 It is very rare to see the Cham dancers unmasked. I was lucky to see these two waiting in one of the little yards behind the monastery.

page 40-41 The perimeter wall of the monastery is considered sacred by the pilgrims; here a group bow to some passing monks.

page 43 On the morning of the first day of the Grand Summons, the vast *thangka* portraying the image of the Buddha is carried from the monastery by a hundred selected monks (on the left). Tibetan cowboys ride beside it to ensure that no one touches it before it is unfurled down a nearby hillside.

page 44 top Monks of the Yellow Hat sect rhythmically beat their drums to accompany the Cham dancers.

page 44 bottom Nomadic pilgrims from the grasslands lower their heads in acknowledgement at the arrival of the Living Buddha in the forecourt of the monastery.

page 47 The Cham dances start around midday, and continue unabated for about six hours. Massive horns herald the start of each highly choreographed dance. The monks remain sitting throughout, while the town's secular officials stand in attendance behind.

The Grand Summons lasts four days and, throughout the festival, pilgrims are continuously walking the path of prayer around the monastery. This 'pilgrims' way', 3 kilometres long, is lined with 1174 prayer wheels, some brightly painted with images of the Buddha, others shimmering gold in the sunshine. The pilgrims spin each prayer-wheel as they pass, the more devout falling onto their knees and then their stomachs at each wheel, clapping their hands and murmuring a brief prayer. The squeaking of the revolving wheels echoes all around the precincts of the monastery, a constant background to the ceremonial.

Early on the morning of the first day of the festival, one hundred Labrang monks carried from the monastery an immense furled *thangka* – an image of the Buddha painted on a cloth big enough to cover the Centre Court at Wimbledon. With much pomp, blaring trumpets and booming conch shells, the *thangka* was transported through the narrow streets to a hill outside the town, accompanied by Tibetan cowboys in fur coats and hats astride small sturdy ponies. There, in the presence of The Living Buddha, the entire community of monks dressed in cerise tunics with yellow shawls, and the thousands of pilgrims, the *thangka* was slowly unfurled down the hillside. Pandemonium ensued at such a wondrous sight, but the monks have a novel form of crowd control to prevent the *thangka* being desecrated by the frenzied pilgrims. An enormous lion, made from papier mâché over a wooden frame and manned by two figures inside it, wove through the crowd, its huge head rearing up and scattering anyone foolish enough to get too close to the Buddha's image.

There had been no snow in Xiahe for more than two years, but the next morning the temperature rose slightly and as we walked to the monastery, flakes began to fall. Already the forecourt was swarming with hundreds of excited families, sitting cross-legged on the ground clad in fur hats and thick coats, anticipating the high point of the festival: the Cham Dancers. The air had an all-pervading smell of yak butter, one of the staple ingredients of the nomad diet. The crowd-controlling lion patrolled to ensure that nobody strayed over the threshold of the forecourt…and we sat on the ground and waited. Then, around midday, there came from within the monastery a repeated deep, resonant boom reminiscent of Hagen calling to the Nibelungen in Act II of Wagner's *Götterdämmerung*. This heralded the appearance of what I took to be secular officials, but what a jaw-dropping sight: with arms akimbo, they walked in solemn procession into the forecourt clad in the most exquisite embroidered and brocaded fur-trimmed tunics with fur hats and mukluk-style boots. They were followed by the cerise-robed monks, wearing *pandit*, the yellow hats of the sect, and carrying painted drums. At the tail end of this many-splendoured parade was The Living Buddha, who took his place on a throne placed on a balcony overlooking the proceedings.

The Wagnerian trombones, well over two metres in length and supported on wooden trestles, boomed out again. A line of drummers took position to one side of the courtyard facing a line of monks with cymbals. Each began a rhythmic beat, the incessant clashing of the cymbals ringing out as the first group of dancers appeared. In all, thirty-five masked and costumed monks danced throughout the day as the soft, stinging snow fell. The story they told was of the battle between Good and Evil, with the leading role taken by Yama, the Lord of Death. The crowd were silent, hynotised by this extraordinary spectacle, and we felt immensely privileged to be spectators to this auspicious marking of the Tibetan New Year.

The history of Antigua, the former capital of Guatemala, is a history of over four hundred years of destruction and devastation, volcanic eruption and violent earthquakes. The early settlers were a hardy lot. After a cataclysmic earthquake in 1541, they set to rebuilding on almost the same site, constructing a city that rivalled Mexico City and Lima in terms of size and importance. But further earthquakes hit the city, including a monumentally destructive one in 1717. The skills of earlier master builders must have been lost, for the latter half of the eighteenth century saw a frenzy of ecclesiastical building in a style referred to by the American architectural writer Sydney Markham as 'Earthquake Baroque'. By 1773 the city supported thirty-one churches, serving a population of just 35,000 inhabitants.

On Saint Martha's Day, 29 July 1773, a violent shock jolted the city, followed about ten minutes later by a massive explosion. The earth convulsed for fully two minutes, then stopped as suddenly as it had began, leaving thousands dead or homeless. Two substantial aftershocks struck before the year was out, finally convincing the Guatemalans to rebuild their new capital some 40 kilometres further east. The old city, which Philip II of Spain had called in 1566 'the very noble and very loyal city of Saint James of the Knights of Guatemala', became officially Antigua Guatemala – Old Guatemala. It survived a further two hundred years of tremors until the mother and father of all earthquakes hit the city on 4 February 1976: in just thirty-nine seconds an immense convulsion killed 35,000 people and made a million people homeless.

Despite this cycle of devastation and reconstruction, the power of the church remained strong through the centuries, and over Easter thousands of purple-robed penitents journey here from all over Guatemala to participate in Holy Week. The crumbling ruins of the monasteries, convents and churches of Antigua Guatemala provide a historic backdrop for the processions that commence solemnly on Palm Sunday and become more elaborate as the week progresses. Good Friday, the day of Jesus's sentencing and death, is the climax of this living theatre of the passion and death of Christ. The tens of thousands of celebrants are at a peak of excitement, as they prepare to witness the unfolding of a moving drama.

At dawn, Roman horsemen and centurions charge through the streets, calling out the sentence for Jesus's death. Meanwhile, thousands of men and boys are gathering in front of the church of La Merced, where the *anda* – a huge float containing the life-sized figure of Christ bearing a golden cross entwined with a silver vine – has been made ready. Eighty of the sturdiest men, who have been specially selected, heave the 3-tonne bier onto their shoulders and commence a swaying march to the accompaniment of sombre chanting. Amid rolling clouds of incense they process through the cobbled streets of Antigua Guatemala and along the fourteen Stations of the Cross. The previous night the entire route has been painstakingly laid with *las alfombras de flores*, 'carpets

of flowers' made from pine needles, coloured sawdust, flowers and grains, whose beauty lasts only for as long as it takes for the procession to trample over them. The spectacle lasts well into the night and there is a distinct impression that little has changed in Antigua since the Spanish first brought Catholicism to Latin America six hundred years before.

Meanwhile, 150 kilometres away to the west, another extraordinary festival is simultaneously taking place. Aldous Huxley was moved to call Lake Atitlan, situated at an altitude of about 1500 metres in the Guatemalan highlands, the most beautiful lake in the world. Reflected in the waters are the three smoking volcanic peaks that ring the lake, and the mirror-like surface changes its hue and mood to match the ever-changing shades of the sky – from dusky blue to pink to grey. The twelve villages around the lake are populated largely by the descendants of two Indian tribes who pre-date the Spanish conquest, and who still speak their own languages and are differentiated by their distinctive embroidered jackets and striped trousers.

Every Easter a part-pagan, part-Catholic ritual takes place on Santiago Atitlan, an island situated squarely in the middle of the lake. Christians the world over mourn the death of the Living God on Good Friday. Then, three days later, they celebrate the Risen Christ. On Santiago Atitlan, the Tzutujil Indians go one step further by fêting Maximón, a transmogrification of Judas Iscariot, the betrayer of Christ. By making offerings to him, drinking his health and pouring out their troubles to him, they neutralise his power and make him safe for the rest of the year.

Maximón, also called Saint Simon, has Mayan origins and is the most revered of the local saints. The source of the evil reputation of Maximón/Judas is uncertain but it may have been propaganda spread by early colonialists, to try to suppress the villagers' fondness for him. Another theory is that Maximón was an Indian holy man whom the conquistadors put to death as they feared his influence. Whatever his origins, the Indians are extremely attached to Maximón, although the authorities discourage his popularity, and official festivals in his name are now confined to just a few villages in these remote uplands of Guatemala.

During the previous twelve months, Maximón's body has been kept in the village by members of the local *cofradía*, or religious brotherhood. Maximón is considered to be too powerful to be kept complete, so, bizarrely, his body parts are kept separately by members of the *cofradía* and he is only 'made whole' by the *telinel*, a shaman or witch doctor, on the Wednesday of Easter week. The next day, in the incarnation of the treacherous Judas Iscariot, he is strung up on a crucifix until Good Friday. Meanwhile, his wife, known as Maria Castellanos, appears in the form of a sacred bundle topped by a mask and shawl. During Holy Week, she lies in a glass case in the home of the same *telinel*. The Atitecos, the villagers, watch over Maximón day and night, bringing him gifts of clothes, money, candles, alcohol and cigars in return for answering their prayers.

On Good Friday, Maximón is taken down from the cross and, dressed in his western clothes and sunglasses and 'smoking' a fat cigar, is lifted high above the heads of the villagers and carried from the home of one *cofradía* member to another. At each house, through to the dawn of the following day, he is toasted with liberal quantities of *quezalteca*, the local fire-water, and villagers, themselves well dosed with *quezalteca*, animatedly pour out their troubles to him as their own father-confessor, bemoaning their lot in life and asking him to fulfil their wishes.

**page 48-49** Villagers from the *pueblos* around Lake Atitlán are distinguished by their embroidery patterns, particularly on the women's *fajas*, which serve as shawl, papoose or 'carry-all'.

**page 51** As the *anda* which bears the lifesize figure of Christ is carried along the main streets in Antigua, the scene is reminiscent of a lavish biblical epic from the early days of Hollywood.

**page 52-53** Clouds of incense waft in front of the *anda* as it is carried over the most beautiful yet ephemeral *alfombras de flores,* created overnight.

**page 55** top It is an honour to be appointed to guard the enormous *anda*, which takes eighty of Antigua's sturdiest men to carry.

**page 55** bottom In the wake of the *anda*: the scattered remains of an *alfombra de flores*. Devotees lining the route of the Stations of the Cross wear tunics of purple, the colour that represents Christ's agony.

**page 56-57** Passions ride high as the villagers of Santiago Atitlan pour out their troubles to Maximón who, they believe, has it in his power to grant their wishes.

Unlike most of the festivals in this book, my visit to the Ganguar Festival was not planned; it was simply serendipity that it coincided with a private visit to the palace of His Highness the Maharana of Udaipur. Maharana Udai Singh founded the city of Udaipur, part of the kingdom of Mewar, on the advice of a prominent spiritual leader in 1559. Its vast palaces and lakes, set amid the Aravali mountains, are simply stunning (the James Bond film *Octopussy* used the city as its principal location) and the tradition of colourful festivals here has continued for centuries. Indeed, the British historian Colonel James Todd wrote in his *Annals and Antiquities of Rajasthan* (1829) that the Mewars had 'a special genius for festivities'.

The festival of Ganguar in Udaipur is very small in size compared to the great *melas* of the Kumbh or Pushkar (see pages 22 and 224) but no less eye-catching. People gather at the *ghats*, the bathing steps, of the old town to honour Gauri, or Parvati, the consort of Lord Shiva. Shiva alone denotes male energy and reproduction, but Shiva and Gauri/Parvati together represent family and

the growth of the human race. Married women worship Gauri for the welfare, happiness and longevity of their husbands, while single women look to her for guidance in finding their life partner at the festival – unmarried girls are required to fast, eating just one meal a day for the whole eighteen-day period of the festival.

At an auspicious hour, clay images of Gauri and Isar (as Shiva is called here) are transported around Lake Pichola on large ochre-coloured rowing boats. The images, gorgeously painted, dressed and bejewelled, are created by artists known as *matherans*, and are accompanied on their journey by young girls attired in their finest saris, their hands and feet decorated with intricate geometric patterns in henna. As the boats slowly drift across the lake, the girls on board dance and chant songs relating to the time when Gauri left her own home to visit that of her husband, Isar/Shiva.

As the sun begins to dip behind the mountains, and the walls of the old city glow in the golden light, the boats reach the waters below the *ghats*, which by now are a riot of multi-coloured shimmering reflections of the thousands that are assembled there, some in the water, others on the steps – hoping that this day will bring them a husband, or a happy married life in the future.

**page 58-59** Young dancers accompany images of the gods Gauri and Isar across Lake Pichola. The painted effigies are seated behind the oarsman.

**page 60-61** All Udaipur gathers at the *ghats* in the old quarter of the town to honour Gauri. Ganguar is a highly festive occasion because it is an opportunity for unmarried women to find their future husbands.

praznik cevera, murmansk

For 35 roubles I had obtained a 'passage in soft sleeping car FAST TRAIN' (their capitals, not mine) on the Moscow–Murmansk Express. Soft the compartments in the German-built carriages might be, but fast the train most certainly was not. It trundled the 2095 kilometres due north at a speed of no more than 55kph across an unrelentingly flat and desolate snow-clad plain for two nights and a day to its destination. Murmansk, officially founded only in 1916, is the largest city in the world within the Arctic Circle and owes its very existence to the Gulf Stream, whose warm waters keep the port ice-free all year round. Its name in the local Saami language means 'the edge of the earth', an apt description, for there's nothing between it and the North Pole other than the Arctic Ocean.

It was late March and I'd been invited to attend Murmansk's Praznik Cevera, or Festival of the North. The official brochure described the festival as: 'a bright example of the great consideration of the Party and Government about the health of the people of Arctic Russia, and their harmonic development in the different conditions of the North.' But although Praznik Cevera was only established during the Soviet era, it evokes gatherings on the tundra in past centuries, when nomadic clans would meet to trade, swap news and hold tests of strength and ability. The festival traditional signals the end of the Arctic night that lasts fifty-two days, and the coming of spring in Russia's Far North. In reality, however, spring does not arrive until June.

An estimated 75,000 spectators had turned up at the Dalina Uyut, the Valley of Comfort, on the outskirts of the city for five days of festivities. For most, the biggest draw was the sport of *beg olenych upraschtschenije* – reindeer racing.

This is dominated by two tiny minority tribes of Lapps, the two thousand-strong Saami and their closely related neighbours, the Kohmi. Both live on the tundra of the Kola Peninsula and believe that they lived in the region even before the Viking culture had been established. Two thousand years ago the Lapps hunted over a vast area of northern Europe, eking out an existence in the impossibly harsh conditions of the frozen tundra. Then, about six hundred years ago, they acquired some knowledge of farming methods from the Norwegians, particularly in the partial domestication of the reindeer, and gradually changed their lifestyle to follow these migratory animals, moving with the herds as they grazed from their wintering areas to the summer pastures. (In the nineteenth century a ban was put on reindeer herds crossing territorial boundaries and the Lapps were forced into deciding in which country they wanted to graze their stock permanently: Sweden, Norway, Finland or Russia's Kola Peninsula.)

Ivan Ivanovich Chuprov is a Kohmi, a reindeer breeder working on the Sovhors Tundra Farm, 200 kilometres from Murmansk. He's earned the title of Master of Sport and has been competing at the Praznik Cevera for as long as anyone can remember – he had been Champion for the previous four years. The track on which he will be defending his title this year has been staked out with

**page 60-61** The champion Ivan Ivanovich Chuprov drives his team of reindeer through a blizzard in the misnamed Valley of Comfort.

**page 63** Clad in reindeer skins against the bitter cold, a Saami woman tends to her flock of reindeer while waiting for her turn to race. In the Praznik Cevera races men and women compete against each other.

**page 65** A Kohmi woman wears a fur-trimmed woollen cape over her traditional reindeer skin clothes. For racing, the reindeer usually have their horns removed to make them more docile.

twigs on a gigantic frozen lake. The course is oval, 1.6 kilometres in length, and competitors, both men and women, are required to complete two laps of the circuit in order to qualify for the next round. The sledges they pull are about 2.5 metres long and nearly a metre wide, constructed entirely of wood and bound together with reindeer sinew. Waxed runners extend from end to end of the sledge in one glorious upward-sweeping line of birch and the driver balances on a simple reindeer-skin seat attached to one end of the frame. Reindeer drew sledges long before horses were harnessed and a single animal can pull a load of around 130 kilos. Bucks require castration before they can be adequately domesticated and driven in harness.

The Saami and Kohmi drive their reindeer in teams of four abreast, charioteer fashion, enabling driver and sledge to hurtle around the deeply drifting snow-blanketed circuit at speeds that can hit 50kph. Competitors are timed individually against the clock, so speed is what wins races. However, reindeer are exceedingly timid creatures, easily frightened and prone to stampeding – frequently they will back into the crowds, inextricably tangling their harnesses.

The racing takes place over three days, and while I was there each day was more fiercely cold than the one before. Blizzards reduced visibility to less than 20 metres, while the temperature dropped steadily to −30°C, causing icicles to form on the eyebrows of the drivers.

The Saami and Kohmi are mostly short, stocky and fair, descended, it is said, from an Arctic Caucasian people who dressed from head to toe in reindeer skins. Today it seems that almost nothing has changed. The men still wear reindeer leggings and upturned-toed moccasins, a long curved knife scabbarded in reindeer leather at their waists. The women dress in calf-length reindeer tunics with mitts attached to the sleeves, the whole capped by a fur bonnet and an A-line woollen cape belted at the waist. As the snow flurries continued to blanket everyone and every creature with cottonwool-ball-sized flakes, the scene took on a timeless quality.

Blizzard or not, the reindeer racing continued, Saami following Kohmi, man following woman. But Ivan Ivanovich was no longer leading the contest. A Saami herdsman called Alexei Terenteyev had taken the lead with a time of four minutes dead. Did Ivan Ivanovich consider this to be an unbeatable time? 'I've no speedometer,' he muttered laconically, 'but I've trained my reindeer especially for this event. I've even removed their horns.'

And with that, he harnessed up his leading animal, Lehzinko, and with much whooping and stick-waving set off for his final gallop around the track. Within a few seconds he was out of sight, veiled by a curtain of snow. Terenteyev anxiously peered through the murk, mentally driving himself through the race, his eyes riveting on any movement that might signify the progress of his rival. At last Ivan Ivanovich appeared on the straight, leaping up and down and willing the animals into one final burst of energy. Suddenly, another Kohmi ran out on to the track, arms flailing wildly, screaming 'He-He!' The animals, apparently panicked by this tactic, almost exploded across the finishing line, nostrils flared, tongues lolling from their mouths, hearts pumping madly. Frozen perspiration rimed the exposed parts of Ivan Ivanovich's face. But he was smiling. According to the other competitors, it was a very fast time. Then the announcement: '3 minutes 59.3 seconds.' Ivan Ivanovich Chuprov, Master of Sport, was Champion for the fifth successive year.

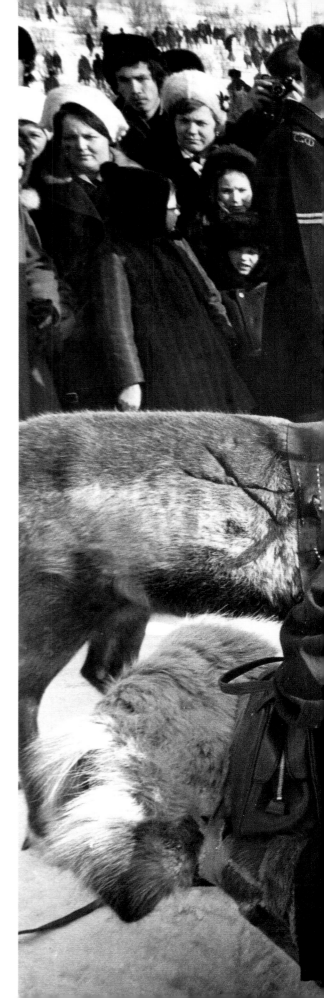

For many, the name Vietnam still conjures up images of a land torn apart by a controversial war, its forests defoliated and its countryside pitted by countless craters from years of American bombing. 'War' and 'Vietnam' seem inseparable in the minds of the world at large. Indeed, the most popular souvenir to be found now in Vietnam is a 'genuine' ex-US Marines Zippo lighter retrieved from some fox-hole on Hill 278.

However, the reality of Vietnam today is very different, and much more enticing. In my view, it is the most beautiful country in South-East Asia – green beyond belief, with neat rice paddies tended from dawn to dusk, extraordinary grottoes buried amid soaring mountains, an immensely lovely and virtually deserted coastline and a quite surreal archipelago of limestone islands scattered across Halong Bay, close to Hanoi.

'The Land of the Ascending Dragon' is also a country steeped in tradition, with a cultural ancestry that can be traced back some four thousand years. I went there, of course, for a festival, of which Vietnam has an astonishing number. The largest and most varied of them occur in the north of the country – in what had been, prior to 1976, the Democratic Republic of North Vietnam. Until recently a request to attend any festival had to be presented to the Tourist Authority in Hanoi a minimum of three months prior to the event, but nowadays the Ministry of Culture is much more relaxed about visits.

The precise dates of Buddhist festivals are determined by the position and phases of the moon, so knowledge of how the lunar calendar functions is a necessary requirement. I'd set my sights on the most inspiring of all northern festivals, Huong Tich, which falls during the first lunar month, which upon calculation turned out to be in April. The location for the festival is the range of mountains south-west of Hanoi known as Huong Son, the Mountain of Perfumes.

I set off one afternoon by minibus from Hanoi, staying the night in a former communist rest-house in Hoa Binh. Although I had made an earlier reservation, this had been outranked by visiting party officials who had commandeered the only en-suite rooms, leaving the rest of us to fight it out over the remaining sparsely furnished accommodation and communal washing facilities. Looking in on the dining room, with its two immensely long trestle tables laid with plastic plates and cutlery, I decided against joining the delegation of four hundred apparatchiks for their pseudo-western dinner of meat, onion and two veg.

The next morning, we drove 60 kilometres to the town of My Duc, the starting point for the river journey to Huong Tich, the Perfumed Grotto, where the main festivities take place. The

pilgrimage to the grotto – which many consider to be the most beautiful spot in the whole of Vietnam – commences with the negotiation for the hire of a rowing boat. The town's population seems to consist solely of boatmen and there are hundreds upon hundreds of punts plying for trade along the riverside.

Once underway, we paddled into the gentle currents of the Yen Vi River and began the meandering trip upstream through the fertile plains, paddy fields and jagged limestone mountains bordering the water. The landscape is probably the most magnificent in Vietnam, and on that misty, opalescent morning took on all the qualities of an Impressionist painting or a Japanese watercolour. It was simply exquisite. I stopped on a bridge for a while and watched a never-ending succession of punts go by. That morning it seemed that everyone in the country was afloat: elderly grannies for whom this is a symbolic annual ritual, excited families sharing their punt with dragons or other spirit images, children too young to know they were participating in part of their cultural heritage. Some would hold their hands up in prayer and mouth a blessing to me: *a di da phat* – may Buddha bless you.

The whole mountain area is considered to have a religious importance, and each peak we passed had a significant name: the Crouching Elephant, the Nun, the Rice Tray, the Bronze. For centuries holy men have travelled here seeking nearness to Nirvana, making their homes in the caves and grottoes, and shrines and temples punctuate every hillside.

An hour later we reached the landing stage near the Thien Tru Pagoda – the Pagoda Which Leads to Heaven. Here there's an opportunity to make an offering to the gods. Smoke coiled up into the morning air from a myriad fires on which the faithful were burning money, albeit fake, as a gift to deceased relatives and friends, so that they will be able to spend it in the afterlife.

The next stage of the journey is a 2-kilometre hike up a very steep, unsurfaced mountain path to reach the massive cavern and grotto encompassing the Pagoda of Perfumes of Huong Tich. We passed by more smaller grottoes and then arrived at the Pagoda of Purgatory, where 'souls are purified and sorrows healed'.

At the summit, many thousands had gathered outside the cave, where an ornate script above the entrance proclaimed this to be 'The First Grotto under the Southern Sky'. Legend has it that the grotto was discovered over two thousand years ago, but work on the pagoda inside, dedicated to the Goddess of Mercy, didn't begin until 1575. The eighteenth-century Buddhist Lord Trinh Sam declared the site to be the most important in the whole of the kingdom and today it still remains one of the most spiritual places in the country.

A perilously steep staircase leads down into the darkness of the grotto's interior. Thousands more had gathered here, the flickering lights of their fires fuelling a vista of yet more burnt offerings to the gods. The grotto walls were oozing dampness onto the upturned stalagmites. Many pilgrims rubbed packs of the local currency, dong (real, this time), onto the wet rock walls in the belief that this would bring them good fortune, while others made offerings of fruit, biscuits and other assorted foods, the traditional incongruously mixed with cans of Sprite and Coca-Cola. These offerings would feed the deceased members of their families in the afterlife. Each rocky nook in the cave was bedecked with the shrines of gods to which the pilgrims, chanting in song, addressed their problems and grievances. Seen through the choking, perfumed smoke of burning incense, this was a chaotic yet unforgettable and spiritually uplifting experience.

Provençal legend has it that in about AD40, Mary Magdalene, Mary Jacoby, mother of James the Less, and Mary Salome, mother of James the Great and John, along with their Egyptian servant Sarah, fled Palestine in a small open boat and were washed ashore on the edge of the Camargue marshlands, at the place now known as Saintes-Maries-de-la-Mer – Saint Marys of the Sea. A conflicting story claims that Sarah was a dark-skinned pagan princess already living in the Camargue, who had a vision telling her of the arrival of the Marys. Seeing their struggling vessel, she threw her long red sash out to the craft and towed it to safety.

Mary Magdalene reputedly journeyed inland, but Sarah stayed, tending the other two Marys and the little church that now houses their remains. Sarah has became the patron saint of Gypsies, and each May upwards of ten thousand Romanies come from across Europe in motorised caravans – gone are the days, sadly, of horse-drawn carts and wagons – to venerate the saints, a time for much dancing, guitar playing, feasting and worshipping.

The Gypsies come from many different ethnographic groups. Those from the Catalan and Andalucian regions of Spain converse in a unique dialect, le kalo, and produce the finest bullfighters, flamenco singers, dancers and guitarists, the most famous being the dancer Carmen Amaya and the guitarist Manitas de Plata. The Manouches are characterised by their small moustaches and beards, and used to live mainly in Germany, earning their living as basket-makers. They are also brilliant violinists and musicians – Django Reinhardt was a Manouche.

Pepe Lafleur, considered King of the Gypsies, is a Manouche. Now over seventy, with thirteen children and at least forty grandchildren, he misses the horse-drawn life. Ten years ago he was briefly persuaded to give up his peripatetic life and he and his wife bought a house, but they left it after just eight days. 'As soon as mid-May is here, I feel pulled to Saintes-Maries; like a lover, it's stronger than me. I go and see Sarah at least ten times a day and I'm at all her vigils.'

On the eve of the festival the heat of the candles in the little church makes the metal handrail on the stairs too hot to hold. The statue of Sainte Sarah is now swathed in brilliant white and blue in preparation for her annual outing, and a train of Gypsies drifts silently and reverently past. Some lay flowers and gifts around her, or press their lips, or those of their infants, against her dark face. The following afternoon she is carried down to the sea on the shoulders of four celebrants. 'Viva les Saintes Maries!…Viva Sainte Sarah!' sing the crowds as they surge forward trying to touch her.

After mass the next morning the statues of the two Marys are also jubilantly carried down to the sea, accompanied by Gypsy herdsmen on pure white Camargue horses. The celebrations come to an end that night and the caravans begin their journeys back…I was going to write 'back home' but, as Pepe Lafleur said: 'A long time ago we came from India, but to tell you truthfully, we come from nowhere on our way to elsewhere…for Gypsies a journey has no end.'

page 76-77 In traditional *costume arlesienne*, the townspeople of Arles wait on the beach for the arrival of the procession bringing the Two Marys.

page 79 In triumph, the Two Marys are carried above the heads of the crowds down to the seashore and into the waves. As the priest blesses them, the sea becomes a maelstrom of fanatical worshippers attempting to touch them.

page 80-81 A Gypsy horseman waits patiently outside the church in which the Two Marys and Sainte Sarah reside. When the holy images emerge he will be among the riders to accompany them down to the sea.

page 82-83 Pepe Lafleur and his wife have been participating in the *pélérinage* for over forty years. Nowadays they come in a traditionally decorated trailer, but he misses the days of the horse-drawn caravans: 'I still dream of them at night.' he confided.

la romeria del rocío, andalucia

One Spanish journalist participating in the pilgrimage to El Rocío for the first time described it as being 'very special but unpromotable; part religion, part adventure, part Paris–Dakar rally.'

The annual *romería* at the shrine of the fabled Virgin, the Lady of the Dew, at El Rocío takes place over the period of Pentecost, normally at the end of May. Up to one and a half million people make the 120-kilometre journey from Seville either on foot, on horseback or in swaying, garlanded ox carts, travelling for three or four days along tracks that are rough, dusty and searingly hot.

This is a uniquely Spanish affair, combining elements of both Semana Santa, Holy Week, and a traditional Spanish *feria*, but on a massive scale. There's singing and dancing twenty-four hours a day, and huge quantities of food and drink are consumed. Many rocieros, as pilgrims to El Rocío are called, celebrate for the entire week and will spend considerable sums of money entertaining their family and friends – one group I met said that they'd spent the equivalent of three months' wages just on food. The women dress in traditional flamenco costume while the men have cloth caps, short jackets, black sashes and high-waisted black striped trousers, *pantalones rocieros*, supported by braces; they while away the time unashamedly dancing *sevillanas* and *seguidillas* in the streets.

*Rocieros* consider the pilgrimage to be the high point of their year and are more than prepared to devote their annual savings to it. But despite this huge indulgence and apparent disrespect for what is essentially a religious gathering, they have an unquestioning devotion to the Virgin Mary.

The cult of the Virgin of El Rocío can be traced back to the fifteenth century. When the Islamic Moors overran most of Spain in the eighth century, the Christian populace, fearing the desecration of religious relics and statues, hid them. Since Moorish rule lasted for over five hundred years, longer in parts of Andalucia, many relics remained concealed, often forgotten, until they were accidentally rediscovered. Often, such discoveries were said to possess miraculous properties.

Legend has it that El Rocío's relic of the Virgin was found under a tree by a hunter from the Huelva village of Villamanrique. He decided to take it back to his village, but fell asleep on the way, and when he awoke the statue was gone. It was later found back in its hiding place and all efforts to take it away failed. Marking the miraculous Virgin's chosen resting place is now the Chapel of the Virgin in El Rocío, and the focus of attention for pilgrims today is this life-sized statue of the Virgin Mary, the Lady of the Dew, holding a figure of Christ and a golden sceptre.

The *rocieros* who make the journey to El Rocío come from all over Spain and from every quarter of society. They all belong to numerous lay Catholic brotherhoods or *hermandades*, and each *hermandad* has its own special house in El Rocío which has been built or rented through members'

donations. The pride of each *hermandad* is the *sinpecado* (literally 'without sin'), a heavy, ornate, silver-encrusted replica of the image of the Virgin, which is carried by ox cart to the festival and which takes pride of place both on the route and in their Rocío house.

These *sinpecados*, each accompanied by hundreds of members of the *hermandad*, set out from villages on the outskirts of Seville some three days before the climax to the pilgrimage on Whitsunday. After an early morning mass in the village square, they set off through the sand and dust, serenaded by the village band. Each *hermandad* party will comprise horses and ox carts, gaily caparisoned, and villagers and *rocieros* shouting 'Viva la Virgen del Rocío! Viva la Paloma Blanca! Viva la Hermandad!' Every twenty minutes or so, the procession stops; rockets and fireworks are set off at key moments and at each major halt, tables are set out with wines and *presunto pata negra*, Andalucia's finest uncured ham – the whole trip seems to be one long gastronomic feast. Later, each party crosses the River Quema in a re-enactment of the biblical crossing of the River Jordan, and newcomers to the pilgrimage undergo a ritual immersion almost comparable to a second baptism. At dusk they finally stop to pitch their tents around the eighty or so ox carts in the group. But there will be little opportunity for sleep as the *hermandades*, in *fiesta* mood, set off fireworks and firecrackers for most of the night.

The last night and day of the journey is spent crossing Las Marismas, a wild and uninhabited area of marsh formed by the estuary of the River Guadalquivir. It was King Alfonso X's royal hunting ground in the thirteenth century and *rocieros* consider the area today to have magical properties, particularly in regard to fertility. As they arrive at their destination, the pilgrims transform the sleepy little village of El Rocío (population 400), which for every other weeks of the years has all the liveliness of a dusty Wild West ghost town.

The climax to the pilgrimage is enacted on the Sunday of this week-long celebration. At an undisclosed time – usually around two o'clock in the morning – the Lady of the Dew (dressed in her summer clothes; she also has a different wardrobe for winter peregrinations) is carried out from the chapel under a silver canopy, carried by eighty sturdy members of the Almonte *hermandad*. Only they are allowed to transport her through the village, and they do an agile balancing act, trying to ensure that she doesn't tilt excessively on her bier as they are rushed and pummelled by the hysterical crowds – all rules of propriety or decorum are set aside in the pandemonium to touch any part of the Virgin.

The bells of the chapel toll, the devotees roar 'Viva! Viva! Vivia!', thousands of firecrackers are set off, and the noise is deafening as the Lady of the Dew slowly begins her twelve-hour progress through the frenzied crowds, visiting every *hermandad* in the village. At each stop, rose petals shower down from the rooftops as pilgrims attempt to reach out to touch her and talk to her. Some are convinced that not only is the Virgin human but also alive. They see tears in her eyes and are certain that she gazes back at them, responds to their cries and will grant to them their every wish.

**page 84-85** All the members of an *hermandad* pose outside their rented house in El Rocío.

**page 87** An *hermandad*, together with garlanded ox-cart, arrives in El Rocío. They set off three days ago for the 120-kilometre walk from their village near Seville.

**page 88-89** Village bands, highly decorated ox-carts carrying the *sinpecado*, a heavy ornate silver-encrusted replica of the image of the Virgin, and flamenco dancers are all essential parts of an *hermandad's* procession to El Rocío.

**page 91** These girls, accompanying the dancers with tambourine and castanets, have a poise and nobility way beyond their years.

**page 92** Dancing in all its forms constitutes probably the single most important element during the festivities of the *romería*. The allure of flamenco, apart from the swinging dresses and obvious excitement of the participants, lies in the undercurrent of restrained passion that runs through the dancing and singing.

# çirit, konya

'He was a fine, athletic type, the best *gereed* thrower in the district. I had taken him into my service as a nightwatchman. Now he had become fatally wounded whilst playing *çirit*. It was difficult to understand how it might be possible to help him. He was quite unconscious on account of the *gereed* which had struck him just in front of one ear and which had gone clean through the neck…'

Edward William Lane, an English adventurer and explorer who travelled widely in the Middle East in the beginning of the nineteenth century recounts the dangers in playing the game of *çirit*. He relates, too, another occasion on which he was witness to how 'three men and a horse were killed in the course of one hour' in this war game.

The ancient equestrian game of *çirit*, thought to have been invented by the nomadic brigands that ravaged and plundered Asia centuries ago, has recently become popular again in Turkey. Both the name of the sport and the weapon with which players are armed, *gereed*, derive from the Egyptian word *djerid* which, taken literally, is a palm frond stripped of its leaves – such palm branches were traditionally used as throwing weapons.

Genghis Khan's mounted Mongol hordes knew of *çirit*, and historical documentation suggests that it was already an established activity in Central Asia as early as 1326. Mounted warriors, with a spear for a weapon instead of a palm frond, used *çirit* as a form of cavalry training.

*Çirit* is a team game. Ten riders, armed with several *gereeds*, make up an *alay* or team. A *gereed* today is about 1.5 metres long and has a rounded rather than a sharpened point, but nevertheless, serious, at times fatal, wounding often results. The two teams each line up on opposite sides of a field which is approximately the size of two football pitches. At a site near Konya, in central Anatolia, I watched *çirit* played in much the same form as Edward William Lane saw it played in Thebes in 1833. This was a competition between teams from the neighbouring towns of Konya and Erzurum, their horsemen keyed up for a game that lasted around two hours. The game revolves around the pursuer and the pursued. Both are armed with a bunch of *gereeds* and, at a speed which is never less than a full gallop, attempt to spear their opponent. Even though *çirit* is no longer played with the same venom as it was centuries ago, it continues to be a dangerous game and on the day I watched many of the players incurred serious head wounds.

In Turkey they say that this is a sport for the bravest of the brave. In the 'good old days' a lawsuit could not be brought against a man who had killed another in *çirit*. However, not everyone suffered their defeat well. The French explorer Antoine Melling wrote in 1899 of the Grand Vizir Youssef Pasha, the Governor of Erzurum, who had an eye struck out when playing. His opponent,

a young officer, was condemned to death. The Vizir later relented, and the young officer received instead a purse containing one thousand gold pieces. However, he was warned that he was never to show himself before the Vizir again.

Today, of course, the aim is to win, not to wound. But the scoring remains somewhat complex. A Turkish expert explained to me how the two mounted referees distribute the points. A hit is rewarded with three points. Catching an opponent's *gereed* in the air also earns three points. *Bagislama* means forcing a disarmed opponent to duck to avoid a feint, and also attracts three points. Maintaining good control over the horse brings a further point, and managing to compete without knocking into any other riders also earns one point. On the other hand, points can also be deducted. Anyone who rides his horse badly, or knocks into another rider, has two points with-drawn. It is also considered cowardly to throw when too close, and throwing from a distance of less than 10 metres forfeits two points. Points appeared to be won and lost with equal alacrity, and the teams from Konya and Erzurum scored 890 points between them.

The game makes great demands on both rider and horse, and requires their mutual coopera-tion. Most of the riders were highly skilled. They were unbelievably good marksmen at distances of well over 25 metres, and this while the horses tore along at full tilt. The seventeenth-century Dutchman Cornelius de Bruyn claimed that he had seen riders throw *gereeds* 100 metres.

The Mongols believed that 'Allah had created Mongols with the same legs that he used when he created the horse'. For the Mongols, the horse was 'the crown of Creation'. And today the hors-es used for *çirit* really are something apart. More like feisty Mongolian ponies, they are bred in the Anatolian countryside and are strong, tough, agile and compact, standing not more than 14½ hands high. Turkish cavalrymen consider them to be almost holy, on the same level as 'the flag, the sword, the bow and the arrow'. The saddles the riders use are styled after old Ottoman battle saddles, with the reins kept very short. I was briefly allowed to ride one and found it to be almost fright-eningly uncontrollable.

On the morning of a game, the horse is groomed and its flanks are massaged with olive oil. It receives oats and half a bucket of water and is then rested until early afternoon. The *çirit* contest is divided into two halves, with a break in between. During this time, the horses have their saddles removed and are rubbed dry with woollen rugs while their legs receive a massage and are washed in cold water.

When the game is over, the players repair to the local tavern – the *chaikhane* – to drink the traditional çirit tea and the horses are led slowly homewards, being carefully exercised for another hour. Strangely, they get no water until the following day, and in the stalls are positioned so that they stand with their heads pointing upwards.

Çirit was a courtly sport while the sultans in Constantinople were in power; indeed, there's still the remnants of a çirit field in the Topkapi Palace in Istanbul. Until the middle of the nineteenth century çirit was played over the entire Muslim Middle East, wherever Turkish influence was at its strongest. When things began to go downhill for the Ottoman court in Constantinople from 1826, çirit went the same way. In 1952, however, the riding club in Erzurum came to the conclusion that çirit deserved to be honoured and respected once again, and reintroduced the game once enjoyed by sultans and vizirs. It is so fast and full of action that it has shown itself to have great appeal, and is given the edge, perhaps, by the chance that players' lives are at times in real danger.

For the Tamil women of Kuala Lumpur, the goddess Amman is their special protector and benefactor, and the festival at which they honour her each July is an astonishingly moving act of homage.

The Hindu Tamils came to the Malay peninsula from Sri Lanka – then Ceylon – and southern India in the nineteenth century to labour in the tea plantations in the Cameron Highlands and on the newly planned rail network. Working conditions were often appalling, and it must have been comforting to turn for help to Amman, or Mariamman, the favoured local deity in many of their villages back home. The Temple of Sri Mahamariamman was constructed in Kuala Lumpur's Chinese quarter in 1873 and there has been a temple dedicated to the goddess on the site ever since. The Tamils, especially the women, worshipped Amman not only because she provided protection from sickness but also from 'unholy incidents', of which there must have been an enormous number in the tea factories and on the railway lines, where production figures routinely counted for more than the safety of the imported workforce.

The festival commences at dawn. Some three thousand barefooted Tamil women assemble on the outskirts of the city, dressed in flame-red saris, garlands of white flowers around their shoulders and balancing on their heads brass jugs containing their offerings of sustenance – fresh milk – to the goddess. As they set off towards the temple they form a remarkable sight, a river of red saris flowing slowly down the fast lane of the motorway that normally brings the rush-hour traffic into the centre of the city.

Their progress through the city to the temple is unhurried. Fuelled by a substantial quantity of a narcotic obtained from chewing betel nuts, the women continuously chant 'Bumptati Buratati, Bumptati Buratati', the repetitive mantra growing in volume and intensity as they near the temple. By the time they reach their destination they are in a high state of drugged intoxication, staring and wide-eyed, their eyes totally unfocused, the corners of their mouths dripping red from the juice of the betel. They are all seemingly transfixed by the need to reach the image of the goddess, kept in the inner sanctum of the temple out of sight from anyone but the devotees, and probably unaware of distractions. However, I felt my presence at this point to be intrusive and retreated to the top of a ladder to one side of the courtyard that framed the inner sanctuary. The scene was extraordinary, as many of the women became hysterical, pushing and shoving and crying out tearfully in their passionate desire to reach the goddess, the Guardian of the Earth, with their gift of milk. But by midday the annual homage was effectively over, the red saris dissipated and central Kuala Lumpur had returned to its bustling, secular norm.

**page 102-103** The Tamil women of Kuala Lumpur, brass jars of milk balanced on their heads, form a balletic counterpoint to the discordance of the Malaysian capital's rush-hour traffic.

**page 105** By the time they reach the inner sanctum of the temple, some of the devotees are in a trance, caused from the narcotic effect of chewing betel nut.

Even in pre-Christian times Croagh Padraig – the Mountain of Patrick – was revered as a holy place and it was probably this attribute, as well as its remoteness, that in due course drew Ireland's patron saint to it. Patrick spent the entire forty days of Lent AD441 on the summit of what was then known as Cruachan Aigil and we can only surmise how arduous it must have been, living probably in a rough-hewn shelter that would have given little protection from the howling gales and storms to which the mountain is prone.

By the eleventh century, Croagh Padraig had become a protected site; indeed, a local chieftain, Aodh O'Conor, had the hands and feet cut off a marauder who preyed on pilgrims. St Patrick's Day, 17 March, became a traditional day of ascent, but after thirty pilgrims were blown off the summit in 1113, pilgrims began to climb the mountain later in the year to avoid the appalling weather, and the main ascent settled on Garland Sunday, the last Sunday in July. Nowadays up to seventy thousand pilgrims annually climb the mountain, some twenty-five thousand on Garland Sunday (or Garlick Sunday as some old-timers still refer to it). Many go barefoot, as Patrick had done fifteen hundred years before.

The day before Garland Sunday was a sunny, cloudless afternoon and we could see Croagh Padraig, or the Reek, as locals call it, standing like a granite beacon 765 metres above the southern shore of Clew Bay. By 5a.m. the next morning, however, the rain was almost horizontal and the wind was howling through the trees. Pilgrims congregating at Old Campbell's – a pub, of course, this being Ireland – were each equipping themselves with an ashwood Reek Staff, an absolute necessity for getting a grip on the loose shale.

The rain continued to lash down, and the pitch darkness was only occasionally split by the faint beam of a torch. As the murkiness of the pre-dawn light was just beginning to clear, an elderly, bald-headed man wearing a long gabardine raincoat materialized in the distance; we could just make out his Reek Staff in his right hand as he picked his way cautiously over the razor-sharp granite shale. As we drew nearer we could see his bare feet were black from an amalgam of congealed blood and peaty earth. This was the sixteenth time, he said in a thick Irish brogue, that he'd made the ascent – and always barefoot. We could only admire his courage.

Towards the summit every few steps resulted in a slither backwards. Progress slowed, too, because of the sheer number of climbers, heads down, intent on reaching the top. Eventually the track levelled out but in the thick mist we were unaware for some moments that we had finally reached our goal. To the right was Patrick's Bed, a large circular group of rocks around which pilgrims were walking clockwise chanting Hail Marys: 'Holy Mary, Mother of God…', and in the distance was the outline of the white stucco chapel, which would be the focus for a mass blessing for the bedraggled but elated pilgrims.

page 106-107 The steep-sided slopes of Croagh Padraig consist of sharp and slippery granite shale. By alpine standards the mountain is not particularly high, but it's a hard climb, not least because of the often inclement weather causing rain and very high winds. A 'Reek Staff' is essential for balance.

page 109 Many pilgrims climb the mountain in bare feet. The distance to the summit and back is about 10 miles, yet despite the sharpness of the stones that surface the route of the ascent, most of them suffer neither cuts nor pain. I tried to overcome the suffering of bare feet but found the pain overwhelming after a few minutes.

page 110-111 Close to the summit the path becomes an incline of 45 degrees and climbers struggle to maintain their balance as the wind buffets them.

The Minho, in the north-west corner of Portugal, is one of the country's most mountainous and greenest provinces. Bounded by the sea on the west and the Spanish province of Galicia on the north, it is, in the words of the sixteenth-century poet António Ribeiro, 'the garden of Europe planted by the sea'.

The Minhotos are the most resilient and spirited of all Portuguese, and highly religious – there are so many *sanctuarios*, or shrines, here that the area has come to be known as The Holy Mount. Every tiny village, however remote in this remote region, has a *romaria* (religious festival) and, particularly during the summer months, the Minho seems to be the scene of a never-ending round of celebrations and of pilgrims on the way to one shrine or another. A major date on the sacred calendar is 15 August, the Feast of the Assumption, which celebrates the assumption of the Virgin Mary into Heaven.

One of Portugal's strangest Assumption Day festivals takes place in the small mountain-top village of São Bento, perched on the hillside just 10 kilometres from the Spanish border and overlooking the lakes of the Gerês National Park, considered to be the most dramatic natural landscape in Portugal.

The mountains of Gerês have for centuries been home to a sturdy, independent people – in the days of the Portuguese monarchy, for example, they paid no taxes to the king at all, beyond an annual tribute of three greyhounds, and for many *minhotos* the walk to the shrine of São Bento is not only a penance to put in order their accounts with the powers above, but a demonstration of their hardiness.

São Bento da Porta Aberta – Saint Benedict of the Open Door – is a truly Minho style of *romaria*. For two days beforehand pilgrims, many of them walking barefoot, begin to converge on this mountain sanctuary, which has been a beacon of devotion since 1758. Dr Acacio Rodrigues, drafted in from the medical school of Oporto University to attend to the needs of the pilgrims, told me that many walked from as far as Braga, a round trip of some 100 kilometres. And temperatures of 40°C are not uncommon in August. I heard of an octogenarian who walked from Braga to São Bento and back in a day, refusing either to eat, drink or talk for the twenty hours of the pilgrimage, and of a young mother who collapsed on arrival at the sanctuary, yet refused any medical assistance as she had to return home that night, a distance of nearly 80 kilometres, to breastfeed her young child.

The minimum requirement for pilgrims is to crawl on bended knees twice around the perimeter of the church, marked out by a granite-faced path blackened by the smears of blood shed from the knees of countless thousands of the devout. But many continue for hour upon hour, right through the night, or until the pain becomes unbearable. One young woman I saw continued to

page 112-113 and 115 The seventeenth-century church of São Bento, emblazoned with *azulejo* tiles, has been a centre of devotion since 1758. Pilgrims are required to crawl twice around the perimeter on bended knees; however, many continue this penance all day – and little appears to have changed in 250 years.

page 116 and 117 Close to the church in São Bento is a shop with unusual wares among the candles and votive offerings: waxen images of body parts. Pilgrims have these blessed and carry them on their penitential circuits of the church.

page 119 An enormous image of the Virgin of Aparecida, the largest of any in Portugal, is carried by forty bearers down the steps of the church in the village of Senhora Aparecida.

page 120 and 121 A timeless image: the boys and girls participating in the Romaria de Póvoa do Varzim create an angelic retinue, yet they are enjoying themselves just as the parents and grandparents did as children before them.

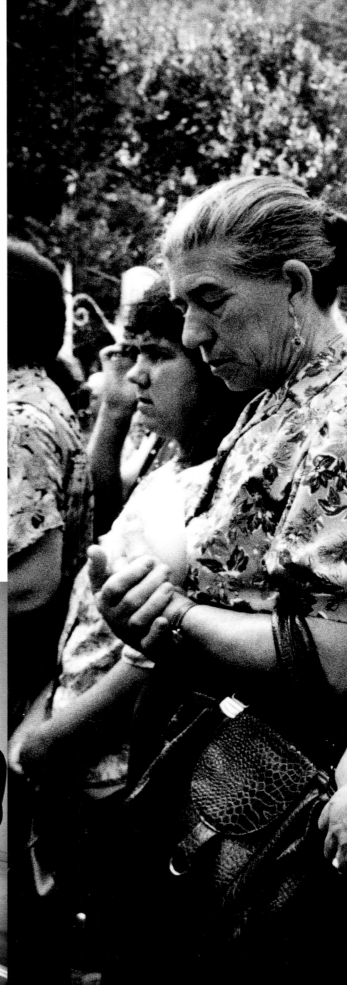

crawl along the bloodstained path throughout the hottest part of the day, until the pain of her ordeal overcame her. She leant on her wooden staff, weeping in agony, trying to take the pressure off her knees. A priest told her that her sacrifice had been sufficient and that the Lord did not want her to suffer further, but she insisted on continuing 'because of her husband'.

Making the circuit with an effigy of an afflicted body part will, it is believed, bring succour, so some circumnavigate the shrine carrying life-like waxen models: some carry a leg or a hand, others an arm, a stomach, even a complete life-sized torso. One elderly woman walked briskly around the shrine for over an hour clutching the image of a cow. The Portuguese word for 'wart' is the same as that for 'carnation', so many also bring bunches of carnations as a gift for 'São Bentinho' for having cured their warts.

But this pilgrimage is not all pain, for, as is the custom in the north of Portugal, celebration accompanies devotion, and the overriding impression of this *romaria* is of non-stop music and dancing. In the woods surrounding the shrine picnickers quaff huge quantities of *vinho verde* from litre mugs, Gypsies swathed from head to toe in black – looking more Balkan than Iberian – barbecue chickens on open fires, exhausted revellers shelter from the searing heat of the summer, and penitents ceaselessly crawl around the shrine. It is an extraordinary three days.

This same mixture of the sacred and the profane characterizes an extremely ancient pilgrimage to the village of Senhora Aparecida, just an hour's drive from São Bento. Centuries ago, so legend has it, a shower of stars fell on this spot and was followed by a miraculous appearance of the Virgin Mary. An important rural fair precedes the *romaria*, and the tiny streets become packed with a mêlée of both horse traders and the faithful. Even during the afternoon of the *romaria* horse races are run along a narrow track formed by the pilgrims!

The culmination of the Romaria da Senhora Aparecida is undoubtedly the procession on the second day, when a statue of Nuestra Senhora is hoisted onto the largest and heaviest bier in the whole of Portugal and manhandled along the steep cobbled streets by more than forty bearers. The faithful kneel along the streets in silence as the image passes them by.

The Virgin Mary is also Our Lady of the Sea, and the seaside resort of Póvoa do Varzim dedicates Assumption Day to the fishermen of northern Portugal. The fishermen, a closed brotherhood steeped in superstitious and religious belief as only those at the mercy of the raging seas of the North Atlantic fishing grounds can be, gather for a huge procession on 15 August. During the *bacalhau* (cod) season each boat leaving Póvoa has carried a special net (the Net of Our Lady), and the proceeds from this 'catch of Our Lady' is used to provide favours for the heavenly protectress of the seamen of Póvoa.

At 4p.m. images of the seamen's patrons are carried through the town on the shoulders of the fishermen. The townsfolk hang carpets from their balconies and shower the fishermen with rose petals as they pass beneath – the procession is so huge that it takes almost an hour to pass by. On reaching a point close to the sea, the fishermen halt and rest their burdens and the Archbishop of Braga, protected from the sun by a white awning, blesses both boats and sailors, to the accompaniment of a seemingly endless and deafening cacophony of firecrackers. Póvoa do Varzim, an unremarkable seaside town at other times, becomes infused with the spirit of Portuguese *romaria*.

I knew very little about the alphorn other than I'd once heard on the radio a sinfonia by Leopold Mozart, father of Wolfgang Amadeus, that contained a virtuoso solo part for this outsize instrument. However, while filming at Neuschwanstein, that fairytale castle built by King Ludwig of Bavaria, I learnt by chance that there was to be an alphorn festival taking place the following day in Nesselwang, a village close to the Austrian border just a short drive away,.

It seemed that every alphorn instrumentalist in Bavaria had come to Nesselwang that morning. There must have been at least a hundred players assembled on a grassy knoll, the barrels of their giant, almost comic, instruments shimmering in the sunshine. Each player was dressed in brown or grey *lederhosen* attached to braces and a leather bib covering their chest, shirts with puffed sleeves and the whole topped by a trilby-like *loden* hat set at a jaunty angle.

During the first part of the morning, groups of players formed themselves into trios and quartets, softly practising a series of arpeggiac chords. The horns have no valves or mechanical keys so all the notes are achieved solely by the position of the embouchure on the mouthpiece. The sound is very deep and tremulous, reminiscent of the lowing of cattle that the instrument had been designed to attract. The alphornists told me that their horns were made from whole trees, specially cultivated on hillsides so that there was a bend at the base. At maturity, the tree was then cut to the alphorn's traditional 'length of two men', split into two halves and carved to shape, the whole process taking about three months. Archeological records suggest that the alphorn existed in a simple form as long as two thousand years ago, and of course there are numerous examples of eighteenth-century paintings depicting the alphorn being sounded by that lonely figure of the alpine countryside – the goatherd or cowherd surrounded by his charges.

The traditional time to sound the alphorn is at sunset, normally an anxious time of day for herdsmen. The instrument makes a unique sound that, through the centuries, has been used for sending signals across alpine valleys. The melancholic notes apparently also had a settling effect on the animals and, over the years, alpine herdsmen built up a repertory of melodies that they exchanged while standing on opposing hilltops.

There was no doubt that the crowning point of the day for the players who had journeyed to the festival was to be part of the Grand Finale. Every alphornist in the region had the opportunity to play in the final harmonic ensemble, and they produced the most glorious, melodious sound that developed almost from a gentle whisper into an enormous series of chords that echoed across the valley. Perhaps this is what inspired Leopold Mozart.

page 122-123 Hundreds of alphorn players assemble on a hill in Nesselwang once a year to play this ancient instrument.

page 125 The size of the alphorn is determined by the ancient method of measuring, the 'length of two men'. The horn can be unscrewed in the middle for ease of carrying.

pogrzebu i triumfu

*Od powietrza, ognia, gtodv i wojny*

*zachowaj nas panie*

From pestilence, from fire, hunger and war,

Protect us Lord

In unison, the repetitive phrases of an old Polish chant dating back some six hundred years rose up from the trees. A group of about fifty teenagers, their heads crowned with thorns, were singing in the pine forests of Kalwaria Paclawska, a couple of kilometres from the Ukrainian border. This was the Funeral and Assumption of the Mother of God, a day of indulgence when all those who participate in the ceremonies believe they can obtain total remission of their sins.

During the seventeenth century, Andrzej Maksymilian Fredro, a Voivode, the Polish equivalent of a Lord High Sheriff, was hunting in the forest when he saw a stag with a cross shining between its horns. This was a message that could not be ignored, and he decided to build a monastery and church on the site, with help from a group of Franciscan monks. The wooden building erected by Fredro in 1688 has been rebuilt in stone, and stands today, almost two thousand feet up, at the very top of a steep hill that rises, pyramid-like, from the fields and River Cedron below. The Voivode believed that the hill bore a remarkable similarity to the Mount of Olives in Jerusalem, so he placed crosses in strategic positions in the surrounding fields and forests, and up the slopes of the hill, to remind pilgrims of the provenance of the True Cross. Over the course of the centuries the original crosses have been replaced by more than forty magnificent stone shrines and chapels which are visited in a specific order by the thousands of pilgrims who trudge the 215 metres up the hill on Assumption Day, 15 August, each year.

Pilgrimages are an integral part of Polish religious life. It is estimated that about eight million people annually make pilgrimages to over four hundred shrines around the country dedicated to the Virgin Mary. Joanna, a Polish friend told me: 'Polish religiosity is almost folksy. You see, it's so much easier to talk to the Virgin Mary than it is to God, because she is everyone's Mother.'

After martial law was declared in December 1981, the Communist regime attempted to eradicate all pilgrimages, especially those on foot, which were considered to be an overly independent form of expression; in retaliation the local authorities would cut the power in the region or would fail to supply bread to the village stores. 'They took our hope away,' Elizabeth, the interpreter said, 'but we still managed to visit these places. Now it's become a tradition to come to these Calvaries. Children are brought here by their parents, as they were brought by theirs. They receive indulgences, they buy souvenirs of the Virgin and make donations to all the beggars; the pilgrimage makes everyone feel good!'

page 126–127  At Kalwaria Paclawska a young pilgrim wears a crown of thorns. Up to four million Poles make pilgrimages to shrines dotted around the country, an increasing number of them teenagers seeking spiritual adventure.

page 129  The Tomb of the Virgin Mary recreated at Kalwaria Paclawska.

page 130-131  On Assumption Day, 15 August, tens of thousands of pilgrims walk the Calvary paths of Kalwaria Paclawska.

page 132  The Palace of Herod, like the other chapels at Kalwaria Zebrzydowska, owes more to Dutch Renaissance style than to the architecture of the Holy Land.

page 133  A group of worshippers bearing a banner of the Virgin stands in prayer just before they reach the summit of Kalwaria Paclawska.

page 134  left  This icon of the Virgin at Kalwaria Zebrzydowska has been recognised for its miraculous powers since 1658.

page 134-135  centre  Mikolaj Zebrzydowski's vision of a Polish Jerusalem underwent much translation in its Eastern European setting: this is the House of Caiaphas.

page 135  right  Christ chained to a column: a sacred image in the cellar of the House of Caiaphas that draws many pilgrims.

Like other Calvaries in Poland, Kalwaria Paclawska was inspired by the first Calvary in the country, begun in 1600 by the Voivode of Kracón, Mikolaj Zebrzydowski. The pious Voivode wanted to recreate a Way of the Cross that would obviate the need for expensive perigrinations to the Holy Land. The previous year one Hieronymous Strzala had brought back from Jerusalem plaster models of the churches of the Crucifixion and the Tomb of Christ, and Zebrzydowski was inspired to use these to begin the construction of Kalwaria Zebrzydowska, in the province of Kracón. Zebrzydowski and his descendants spent the next 102 years laying out over an enormous area of rolling hills and woodland a series of 42 chapels, shrines and other features in imitation of the topography of Jerusalem. Most were designed in the Dutch Renaissance style by the Flemish artist Paul Baudarth, and the first to be built were Golgotha on the Hill of the Crucifixion, and Pilate's Palace in 1605, followed by the Palaces of Herod and Caiaphas in 1609, and the Garden of Gethsemane in 1617. In Zebrzydowski's own personal chapel was placed a painting of the Virgin and Child which as early as 1658 was recognized by the Church authorities as 'famous for miracles' and which is said to have been regularly shedding tears ever since. All the buildings were linked by

Zebrzydowski's own version of the Via Dolorosa, a broad 20-kilometre path that winds up, down and around the hills of his 300-hectare estate. Sadly, it is now half-obscured by weeds.

In Kalwaria Paclawska there had been tens of thousands of pilgrims; the ceremonies at Zebrzydowska attract an estimated one million pilgrims. The atmosphere, though very much a spiritual adventure, is more akin to a marathon than a religious peregrination. Imagine a searingly hot and cloudless day, in which the participants are solely intent on reaching their goal – to complete their walk that day around the entire route of Kalwaria Zebrzydowski, visiting every shrine on the way. Wearing crowns of thorns and singing at the top of their voices, they pass by in groups of thirty or so, each group accompanied by their village brass band and bearing a tall silken banner embroidered with a cross and the name of the region or village from which it started.

Pope John Paul II was born close by, in Wadowice, and made regular pilgrimages to Kalwaria Zebrzydowski. On his visit in 1979 he said: 'What constantly draws people here is this mystery…this mystery which is told artistically and generously throughout the churches and chapels.' The Polish author Michael Rozek amplifies this in his preface to *Mysteria*, by the photographer Adam Bujak: 'The vague border between a sacred mystery and a festive response is often crossed. This particular combination of faith, mysticism and liturgy is continued because religious cults are an important factor joining human communities during their group experience of a festivity, when saints are worshipped, anger is soothed, sins are absolved and peace is made.'

This indefinable sense of mystery could be felt most clearly inside the Church of the Third Fall, the thirty-fourth shrine on the route. The sun was almost at its zenith, and outside it was stiflingly hot without a breath of wind, but inside eddies of colder air drifted down from the domed roof, providing a soothing, but almost chilling, effect. The lavishly embossed gold and gilt baroque interior was in deep shadow, except for an enormous golden cross that lay across the altar, lit like a beacon by the powerful rays of the sun streaming in from the sole window high up on the south wall. Inside there was total silence, save for the echoed murmurings of two women who were crawling around the perimeter of the altar on their knees. A group of villagers just departed were singing the same unaccompanied medieval chant I had heard in Paclawska:

From pestilence, fire, hunger and war,
Protect us Lord.

As their singing became fainter and less defined, another group approaching the church from the opposite direction, from Golgotha, was singing a wholly different chant to guitars and drums:

Oh Holy God, Oh Almighty One,
Holy and Immortal, have mercy on us,
And over the whole world.

We all sat motionless in the sombre darkness, spellbound by the simplicity of the antiphonal sound of the two choruses; this really was a sacred mystery.

page 136  Inset into the 28 steps leading up to Pilate's Palace are particles of the soil of Jerusalem, and the faithful kiss each step, as they crawl up on their knees.

page 137  Pilgrims kneel in obeisance in the Church of the Third Fall, transfixed by this image of Christ's agony, lit by the midday sun.

page 139  At Kalwaria Zebrzydowska the Via Dolorosa ends at the top of the Hill of Golgotha, where a hooded penitent begs.

Siematycze is an anonymous and rather desolate little town in eastern Poland, just a few kilometres away from the border with Belarus. During the Second World War the Red Army invaded the area and the townspeople found themselves inside Soviet territory; many of them were deported to Siberia, never to be seen again. But the lands here are steeped in Russian-Byzantine culture, and their traditions were originally established in about the eleventh century, at a time when conditions were most favourable for the Orthodox faith to develop and flourish in this part of Poland.

Today, time seems to have passed the region by. Hay continues to be transported from the fields by horse and cart, and there are still villages comprised of quaint painted and weathered single-storeyed wooden cottages. Storks nest on the tops of telegraph poles and the ubiquitous cardboard-bodied Trabant car remains a principal form of motorized transport. But the Russian influence is most evident during August, for in this remote border country lies the largest centre of pilgrimage for Poland's one million members of the Orthodox Church. At the time of Przemienienia Panskiego, the Feast Day of the Transfiguration, tens of thousands of pilgrims make their way from Siematycze along an unsurfaced dirt road leading to Świetą Góra Grabarka, the sacred Hill of Penitents at Grabarka.

On the top of this wooded hilltop, there used to be a nineteenth-century wooden Orthodox church, but it burnt down during the summer of 1990 and has now been rebuilt in brick. What differentiates this hilltop from any other in Europe, however, are the crosses. Many of these penitential crosses have stood on the mount since the eighteenth century; some are as much as 3 metres tall, others are as tiny as a crucifix that might hang around the neck. And there are thousands of them planted in the ground around the chapel, forming a seemingly impenetrable forest of wood. A nun from the nearby convent explained to me that the crosses had been left 'in memory of the sick and the suffering, by those who had been cured and by others who had lost their way in life.'

Pilgrims believe that a wooden cross brought and placed here has the power to fulfil the very purpose upon which the pilgrimage to Grabarka was founded. At the beginning of the eighteenth century a cholera epidemic swept through Poland, and people were dying en masse. Legend has it that in 1710, inspired by a prophetic dream, an old man led his companions up to the top of the mount, each one carrying a cross on his back. Once there, the group prayed and drank water from a nearby spring and, despite the fact that they had come from the very centre of the plague area, none of them died. Even more amazingly, those that were ill were cured. The crosses the group had brought were left as a devotional offering, and soon after the place was proclaimed sacred and the miracle was commemorated by the construction of a chapel. Today, the chapel houses a copy of the famous icon of the Mother of God of Iweria. The original, in the Iwerian Monastery on Mount Athos in Greece, is one of the most revered icons in the Orthodox world (it is said that when the

page 140–141  For almost three hundred years the holy mount of Grabarka, with its thousands of crosses, has been the most important religious centre for the Orthodox faithful in Poland.

page 143  The crosses that have been brought here over the years now form an impenetrable forest of wood carrying messages and tokens of gratitude to the Virgin.

page 144  This monk, awaiting the arrival of the Metropolitan Archbishop of All Poland, could have been a model for a fourteenth-century icon painter.

page 145  Calm and statuesque, a nun conveys the deep sense of religious mystery with which Grabarka is imbued.

page 146–147  The waters that emanate from the Troscianiec spring are considered to be most holy, and after washing in it pilgrims leave their handkerchiefs hanging on the trees in remembrance of their visit.

page 148  As dawn breaks the Metropolitan celebrates mass for a congregation of thousands. His altar is on a small dais that has been erected on the side of the hill and over this holy place rise the powerful voices of an unaccompanied choir.

page 149  Some of the crosses on the hill are over 5 metres high, others barely taller than the blades of grass in which they nestle.

page 150  Pilgrims spend the entire night on the top of the hill resting among the crosses, with food and drink to sustain them throughout the vigil.

page 151  Candles shine out into the darkness of the night, illuminating the church and the penitential crosses.

icon eventually disappears in the same miraculous way in which it appeared, that this will be a sign that the end of the world is at hand). When Grabarka's copy was brought from Greece to its new home it was greeted by 50,000 pilgrims.

The date of the Feast of the Transfiguration is 19 August, but in Grabarka the festivities begin on the eve of the holiday, when thousands of pilgrims stream towards the sanctuary during the afternoon. Their first task is to take a ritual ablution in the narrow rivulet flowing around the base of the Hill of the Penitents. Women wipe their breasts with cloths moistened from it, others drink from bottles filled with water collected from the spring, and I watched an old man, crouched low over the bank, spend many minutes with his right hand immersed in the water. He then carefully dried his hand with a white handkerchief that he placed on the side of the stream to join the hundreds of others that had already been left as a sign of the water's spiritual healing power.

Later in the evening, the upper slopes of the pine-covered hill become the focus of an all-night vigil for the dead. Pilgrims, who have been arriving over the course of the day, cram onto the summit, trying to find the tiniest of spaces among the crosses where they can rest during the cool night. The darkness of the night becomes illuminated by thousands of candles held by the pilgrims, then at midnight, the bells of the chapel begin to peal, summoning the faithful to a *panichida*, a funeral mass conducted by the highest Orthodox dignitaries in the land.

And then, at the dead of night in this extraordinarily sacred place, came the mesmerizing sound of powerful bass voices singing in unison, as Russian incantations rose up from the Orthodox choir, resonating amid the forest of crosses.

Abbots Bromley, in the industrial Midlands, is an ancient village with a history that can be traced back to AD942. A substantial church was built here in Norman times, and subsequently extended during the fourteenth century. Today, this church is the repository for six pairs of reindeer horns of great antiquity which, once a year, are brought out for the Horn Dance, believed to be part of a pagan hunting ritual with origins that can be traced back to early Saxon times.

There is no fixed date for the performance of the Horn Dance, one of all too few English village celebrations that has managed to survive intact from medieval times. However, it is always performed on a Monday and the quirky formula to determine the date is 'the Monday following the first Sunday after the fourth of September'. It's likely that the dance was first performed at the three-day Berthelmy Fair, granted to the abbots of nearby Burton-on-Trent by Henry III in 1226. The fair celebrated St Bartholomew's Day on 24 August, but when the Julian calendar was introduced in 1752, the fair was moved to the beginning of September and the three-day celebration became compressed into a single day.

At around daybreak on the morning of the dance, the horns are blessed in the church's Hurst chapel and then collected by the dancers who start their ritual by dancing in front of the church. From there they move on to the village green, and thence walk – and dance – to outlying farms and villages, ending back at the church at dusk some twelve hours later.

The dancers consists of a group of twelve. Six men carry the heavy, metre-wide reindeer antlers – three white pairs and three black – and the rest of the company is made up of Maid Marion, the Hobby Horse, the Jester or Fool, a Child carrying a bow and arrow, and two Musicians, one beating time on a triangle and the other who in times past played the fiddle, but today plays the accordion. The dancers are, by tradition, all male, and for centuries the Horn Dance has been under the leadership of two local families, the Bentleys and Fowells, another tradition that remains unbroken.

From dawn to dusk the dancers and musicians thread their way around the village and through the countryside, sometimes winding in single file along the country roads, sometimes forming into a circle or pairs or interweaving rows as they measure out the steps of their age-old dances. At intervals the 'stags' draw up opposite each other and charge in mock rutting battles.

Deer still live in the remnants of the once extensive forests around Abbots Bromley, and it would be reasonable to assume that these ancient horns are deer antlers. They are, however, not deer, but reindeer. A carbon dating by Birmingham University in 1976 dates them around 1065, about the time of the Norman Conquest. There is some conjecture as to how they arrived in England but the most plausible explanation is that they were brought over by Vikings. The Humber Estuary, into which the River Trent flows, faces Scandinavia, and at the time offered marine access for Viking boats directly into the heart of the Midlands. The region was invaded by both Danes and

Saxons, and the name 'Bromley' is of Saxon origin, so the reindeer horns could have been shipped to England by Viking boats from either Norway or Denmark, and then transported up the River Trent. The first mention of the Horn Dance, however, does not appear until the seventeenth century, in Dr Robert Plot's *The Natural History of Staffordshire*. He refers to:

> six dancers carrying on their shoulders as many Rainders heads . . . At Abbots, they had within memory celebrated at Christmas . . . the Hobby Horse Dance, from a person that carryed the image of a horse between his leggs . . . and in his hand a bow and arrow [with] which he made a snapping noise as he drew it to and fro, keeping time with the Musick; with this man danced 6 others, carrying rainders heads 3 of them painted white and 3 red . . .

Several historians have compared the Bromley Horn Dance to the deer and buffalo dances of North American Indians. There also references in the Bible to wearing deer horns as a sign of strength, and Shakespeare's *As You Like It* even contains a song relating to the wearing of horns:

> *What shall he have that killed the deer?*
> *His leather skin and horns to wear*
> *Then sing him home.*

On this day, as the Horn Dance wove its way through the villages of rural Staffordshire, this was medieval England, simple and unfettered.

page 152–153  The Horn Dancers approach the Elizabethan manor of Blithfield Hall, which they have visited for centuries on their annual journey around the villages of east Staffordshire.

page 155  After winding single file in a figure of eight, the dancers turn to face each other in pairs, following a dance pattern passed on from generation to generation.

page 156  The horns are kept in the chapel of the parish church of Saint Nicholas, and at dawn are blessed by the parish priest before they are carried out by the dancers.

page 157  Caught in the pre-dawn light, my first view of Abbots Bromley's Norman Church seemed utterly timeless.

page 158–159  The largest of the horns has a spread of over a metre and weighs almost 12 kilos. The food and drink with which the dancers are plied along the route must be welcome sustenance for all their effort.

page 160  left  The Jester or Fool carries an inflated pig's bladder on a stick – touching it is believed to aid fertility.

page 160–161  centre  Although the Horn Dance has been performed for centuries, the costumes the dancers now wear originate from Victorian times.

page 161  right  The route of the dance takes twelve hours to complete and the musicians have no more than the occasional respite from playing.

pages 162–163  The Hobby Horse meets his real-life counterpart, a bizarre scene that both accept with aplomb.

High in Mexico's Sierra Madre, on top of a 2750-metre rocky outcrop called La Bufa, perches the Santuario de Nuestra Señora del Patroncinio. There have been testimonies to the cult of the Virgin of La Bufa since 1589, and for a week each September the old silver-mining town of Zacatecas, at the base of the mountain, resounds with fervent drumming and chanting intermingled with children's laughter, as pilgrims set out to pay the Virgin their respects.

Zacatecas was already a prolific mining town in the sixteenth century and until the mid-1960s used to produce thousands of tonnes of silver a year. It still has the appearance of a town which has grown in fits and starts depending on the price that silver fetched in a particular year. Production must surely have been at its zenith in the mid-eighteenth century, when construction began on the town's stupendous pink cathedral, considered perhaps Mexico's finest colonial building. The perfect square of the baroque Plaza de Armas opens up to the north of the cathedral and it's here that the pilgrims gather each day. Each profession, including bullfighters, painters, carpenters and miners, has its own *gremio* or guild and a schedule announces which guilds are to gather in the square and make the climb to the summit that afternoon. The nominated guilds gather at about four in the afternoon, led by stomping, dancing and chanting *matachines*. The *matachines* wear long aprons colourfully embroidered with mirrors and sequins, and sandals with hard soles that make a loud staccato sound as they dance. On their heads are large, round flat caps made of feathers – a reminder of the time they were purely hunters.

Each group is marshalled by four *capitanes* and El Viejo de la Dansa, a masked clown-like character representing Evil, who whips the dancers into line. He's dressed to both frighten and delight the crowds, and incongruously carries a doll, La Malinche. Legend has it that La Malinche was a native woman who was an interpreter to the Spanish conquistador, Hernán Cortés, and therefore branded a traitor by her own people. Also in the procession is a counter to El Viejo, a small boy dressed as a buffoon, who represents *alegría* or the joy of the dance. He's usually the son of one of the *capitanes*, as the role is a jealously guarded prize handed down through the generations.

El Viejo clowns, frightening and jeering his dancers on, and the children shriek in terrified delight when he chases them around the square. Suddenly a drumbeat announces the departure for the mountain, and the *gremios*, led by their *matachines*, wind their way through the cobbled back streets of old Zacatecas and past crosses draped in white to symbolise peace. A violin, a drum and a flute provide the rhythm for the dance-procession, and each *matachine* brandishes a *guaje* or rattle at each step to the summit. I followed 82-year-old Don Daniel to the summit, admiring him as he unceasingly kept time with his battered old violin, never pausing to take breath in the thin air. I imagine him still, playing exactly the same tune each year as the *matachines*, El Viejo and the *gremios* come together, as they have for centuries, to make the annual pilgrimage to La Bufa.

page 164-165 Don Daniel, 82 years old, makes his way past a Station of the Cross on the way to the summit of La Bufa, as he has done for decades; his violin playing will not cease its simple refrain throughout his climb.

page 167 In a back street of Zacatecas a group of *matachines*, accompanied by Don Daniel, prepare to set off. Among them is a small boy who represents the joy of the dance.

page 168–169 *Matachines* dancing before their climb to La Bufa bring noise and excitement to the Baroque square of the Plaza de Armas in the centre of Zacatecas.

page 170–171 top El Viejo de la Danza hugs to his wizened cheeks the image of La Malinche, a fifteenth-century Indian woman now symbolised by a doll.

page 170–171 bottom A masked *capitán* heads up his *matachines* in the courtyard of the sanctuary of La Bufa, at the end of their afternoon's climb.

fête de saint-michel, normandy

Mont-Saint-Michel, La Merveille de l'Occident, The Wonder of the West, was dedicated to St Michael the Archangel by Aubert, Bishop of Avranches in AD708. In a series of dreams the archangel ordered the bishop to transform this rock off the Normandy coast into a place of worship dedicated to him, and it became one of the most important places of pilgrimage in the western world, alongside Rome, Jerusalem and Santiago de Compostela. A constant flow of myths and legends attached to Mont-St-Michel: that it is the site of the Holy Grail; a centre for astrology and alchemy; where the Knights Templar hid their secrets; and part of a sacred alignment of standing stones running via Delphi and Delos to Mount Carmel.

The warrior-archangel was believed not only to guard the gates of Paradise but also to protect souls on their last voyage to heaven, and in medieval times a pilgrimage to the Mount assured a smooth passage into the afterlife. As today, the pilgrims would bring small lead caskets into which they would scoop sand from the bay. The waters here experience some of the strongest tides in the world – during the spring tides the difference between high and low tide can be nearly 14 metres. The sea can recede 15 kilometres then rush back at a speed of a metre a second, making walking on the expanse of tangue – the sand and mud exposed at low tide – potentially very dangerous. Many early pilgrims were swallowed up or drowned, and the Mount became known as Saint Michael in Peril from the Sea.

For one of the biggest annual pilgrimages, at the end of September, I joined about five hundred barefoot Marcheurs des Chemins du Mont from the Normandy town of Vire. We were led by local guides, coils of rope slung over their shoulders in case of quicksands, and equipped with walkie-talkies. Some 8 kilometres directly south stood our destination, over 150 metres high and breathtakingly beautiful on that autumnal afternoon, silhouetted against a cloudless blue sky. No wonder the Mount is a beacon of spirituality. The tide was so far out that the flats appeared as an infinity of golden desert, and the curvature of the earth could clearly be seen. I spent some years in the Middle East, and to my eye this was more Empty Quarter than northern France. We took a circuitous route to avoid deep gulleys, where the sea remained thigh deep, and arrived at the base of the Mount during the late afternoon. Here we cleaned our feet in a symbolic washing ritual.

That evening, our group had been granted a special vespers in the abbey's chancel. Like millions before us, we were overawed by the architectural splendour as we climbed the twenty-four staircases and 291 steps to reach the Romanesque church on the very summit. Singing has always been a passion of the monastic fraternity here and, while the white-habited nuns and monks of the Brotherhood of Jerusalem intoned their hauntingly beautiful responses, I couldn't help reflect on the precarious state of the world as they sang to Saint Michael, guardian of the gates to Paradise: 'Aidez-nous dans le combat contre les forces du mal' – 'Help us in the fight against the forces of evil.'

**page 172–173 and 175** A group of about five hundred pilgrims make their way south from Bec d'Andaine across the bay towards Mont-Saint-Michel. At low tide, the sea retreats some 15 kilometres, revealing a vast expanse of tangue punctuated by deep gulleys, where it is necessary to wade through thigh-deep sea water.

**page 176** The object of pilgrim's veneration: the silver statue of Saint Michael in the parish church on the Mount Saint Michael, 'the Prince of the Heavenly Host', had very special significance in medieval life, for he was considered to be the guardian of the Gates to Paradise.

**page 177** After their walk across the bay and a ritual washing of their feet the Marcheurs des Chemins du Mont celebrated a special vespers in the Romanesque abbey situated at the very summit of the mount, in a part that is known as La Merveille, the Marvel.

**page 178-179** The rock of Mont-Saint-Michel is a last vestige of a range of mountains formed over 600 million years ago; it is said that the rock has been a sacred place since the period. The first shrine was built on it during the eighth century, the first chapel was constructed between AD900 and 930 and by the year 1000 the Mount was known as The City of God.

Certain towns and cities that hold great religious festivals exercise, I have sensed, an invisible but powerful force on their inhabitants, mesmerising them into an almost hypnotic state during the period of the festivities. This feeling of spirituality is always present yet seems to intensify particularly as dusk approaches, perhaps enhanced by the architectural splendour of the buildings around which many of the ceremonies are enacted. There is no question in my mind that Zaragoza, in north-eastern Spain, exerts this force on the many thousands of pilgrims that come here each year to pay homage to Nuestra Señora del Pilar, Our Lady of the Pillar.

According to local legend, the Virgin Mary, while still living in Jerusalem, miraculously came to Zaragoza to visit Saint James the Apostle, who at that time was living on the banks of the River Ebro preaching the gospel to his early converts. Her visit is said to have taken place on a quite specific date, 2 January in the year AD40, and Zaragozans believe that there are several features that differentiate the Virgin's visitation to their city from any other miraculous appearance. She did not appear as an apparition – as at Lourdes in France, or Fatima in Portugal – but came to Zaragoza while still living in Palestine. She is also said to have brought with her a marble pillar or column, the *pilar* which marked the spot on which the first chapel was built. Indeed, Spaniards have always considered this chapel to be the very first Marian temple in all Christendom.

All the celebrations now focus on the imposing Basílica de Nuestra Señora del Pilar. The first basilica was built early in the fifteenth century but was destroyed by fire in 1443, and the present many-domed Baroque structure that replaced it was completed in 1718. Like its predecessors, the basilica was designed around the Column of the Virgin, which has never been moved from its original site. The sacred pillar, which can just be spied through a circular window, is the object of greatest veneration for the devout believers who come to the basilica. On the other side of the *pilar*, and almost equally venerated, hangs the sumptuously bejewelled image of La Gran Corona de la Virgen del Pilar, encrusted with 2836 diamonds, 5725 rose quartz stones, 145 pearls, 74 emeralds, 62 rubies and 46 sapphires.

For a week every October, Zaragoza is brought to a complete standstill as hundreds of thousands pour into the Aragonese capital to honour the Virgin and her miracle; indeed the local paper, Heraldo de Aragón, estimated that, over the two principal days of 2001 when I was there, at least 500,000 people participated in the various ceremonies. Throughout the festival there is the most extraordinary and striking juxtaposition of the sacred and secular. Enormous papier-mâché *gigantes* and *cabezudos* (big-heads) parade noisily right past the doors of the basilica where continuous mass is being celebrated (and confession can be heard even at four o'clock in the morning), and huge crowds are drawn both to the dancing in the street and to the intoning of the mass behind the basilica's great studded doors.

page 180–181   As dancers and guitarists perform outside the basilica during the *ofrenda de flores a La Virgen*, the overriding sound is that of the dancers' castanets.

page 183   I found the evening ceremony of El Rosario de Cristal the most moving of all the festivities, as columns of chanting pilgrims bear through the city magnificent glass crystal floats etched with polychromatic images of the Virgin Mary.

page 184–185   On most mornings the city is brought to a standstill by the parade of the *comparsa de gigantes*, the troupe of giants. Characters represented by these 5 metre (16 foot) high figures include the King and Queen, Christ and the Virgin Mary.

page 186   left   The bouquets of flowers offered to the Virgin Mary during the *ofrenda de flores* are woven into an enormous pyramid; at the very top is an image of the Virgin of El Pilar.

page 186–187   centre   In the chapel of St John the Baptist, the seventeenth-century image of Christ crucified receives particularly special veneration from the inhabitants of Zaragoza.

page 187   right   On the Thursday of festival week an image of the Virgin is borne from the parish church of San Pablo to the Basilica. The procession, which takes place at five o'clock in the morning, is known as the Rosario de la Aurora.

page 188   Pilgrims with their candles gather outside the Iglesia del Sagrado Corazón for the lantern procession.

page 189   From dawn to late afternoon on the penultimate day of the festival, 370 *cofradías* (brotherhoods) of pilgrims flowed towards La Plaza del Pilar, carrying their offerings for the Virgin; it was a joyous occasion for every one of them.

On the Friday of festival week, 300,000 pilgrims wearing *traje campesino*, the traditional dress of the peasants, come to the city bearing flowers as offerings to the Virgin for the overwhelmingly beautiful *Ofrenda de flores a la Virgen*. Starting at eight in the morning, they continue to pass into the main Plaza del Pilar until mid-afternoon, and the flower offerings are built up into an enormous floral mantle about 15 metres high which almost fills the great expanse of the square. The next night, a further 30,000 pilgrims, in traditional eighteenth-century *traje aragonese* with the women wearing black mantillas over their heads, file through the streets of the city carrying twenty-eight huge glass rosaries – *rosarios del cristal*. Singing the continuous refrain *'Ave, Ave, Ave Maria. Sancta Maria, Sancta Maria'* at the top of their voices they proceed by candlelight through the city to the Plaza where they stop in front of the basilica to pay their respects to the Virgin. The power and devotion of the pilgrims during this ceremony must surely leave a profound mark on all who witness it and I left Zaragoza the next day as uplifted as if it were the first day of spring.

It is early October, at dawn on the eighth day of the ninth lunar month in the Chinese calendar. A woman climbs a ladder some two storeys high, apparently impervious to the pain its razor-sharp treads must surely cause, nor do the soles of her feet shed any blood. Nearby, another woman is walking barefoot across red-hot coals, again seemingly without pain. A little further on, a young man is staring blankly into space, then, as if in a trance, he takes a sword and slowly pierces the side of his face. The blade of the sword passes clean through one cheek and exits through the other side of his mouth – without bleeding.

There is no trickery or magic involved in these bizarre scenes, for this is the island of Phuket, on the west coast of southern Thailand, and the occasion is the town's famous Vegetarian Festival. The devotees who inflict these seemingly horrendous acts of mutilation on themselves are merely participating in the Chinese Song Dao ceremony, the rituals of which stretch back nearly 160 years. These acts of apparent torture, a commonplace feature throughout the ten days of the festival, are performed in the belief that they will achieve great kudos for the sufferers while at the same time freeing them of any spiritual problems and bring them a trouble-free year. For the period of the festival, participants wear a white loincloth and smock, cleanse their bodies by abstaining from sex and alcohol, and spend long periods meditating in the town's two main Chinese temples. They eat only vegetarian food that does not contain 'sharp' tastes such as garlic or chillies, and their food must only be cooked using kitchen utensils belonging to devotees who take part in the festival. People in mourning are not allowed to participate, nor are pregnant or menstruating women.

The Song Dao festival is in honour of the Nine Emperor Gods who control people's destinies. Although its origins remain unclear, the festival is thought to have begun during the reign of King Rama V, around the middle of the nineteenth century, when hundreds of Chinese had come to work in Phuket's tin mines. The Chinese immigrants began to neglect their rituals to the gods and, about the same time, the area was hit by a malaria epidemic. When malaria killed off most of a visiting theatre troupe, the actors, being highly superstitious, blamed the arrival of the evil epidemic on the tin workers' neglect of their historical traditions. So an envoy was despatched to China to invite the Nine Emperor Gods, Kiu Ong Iah, to Phuket. Some three years later, the messenger returned to the island bearing an urn containing incense that had been prepared during the invitational ceremony in southern China. On the following ninth lunar month, a ritual celebration was made to the Kiu Ong Iah and the epidemic was wiped out. For Phuket's tin workers Song Dao not only provided a way of honouring the gods but also gave expression to their happiness at surviving an illness that was, in the nineteenth century, fatal. The rituals become an annual event and today the festival, which always falls on the first days of the ninth Chinese lunar month, is the largest in Thailand – but is not recommended for the faint-hearted.

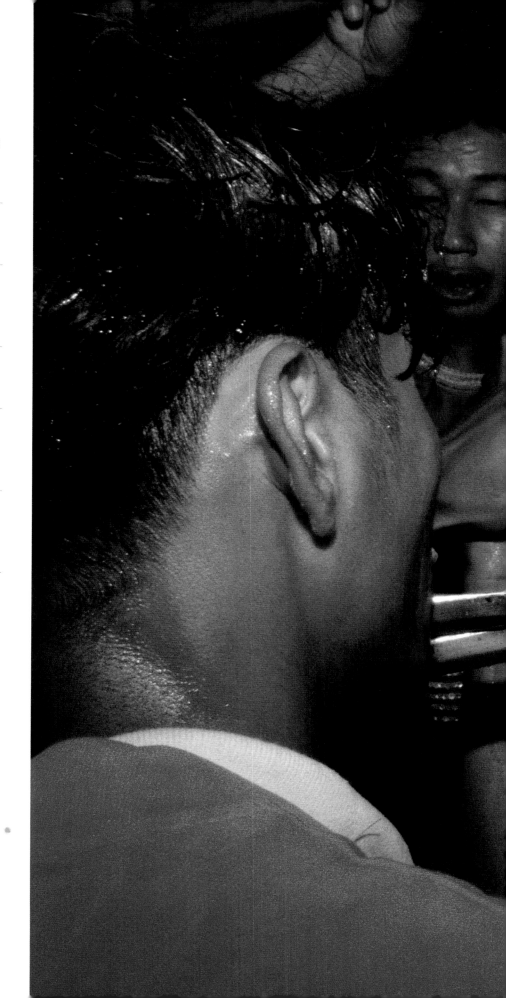

Throughout the festival ear-splitting fusillades of firecrackers are exploded to drive off the evil spirits, and cymbals and gongs announce the daily parade of devotees through the centre of the town. This is a scene of gruesome fascination, for some have their faces skewered by the most monstrous-sized weapons. I saw one who had inserted two model shotguns through his mouth, another the entire branch of a tree, while a third had his cheeks pierced by a pole of incredible length, garnished with apples and supported by willing aides.

But these incredible sights are not the only interesting feature of Song Dao. It is the eighth day of the festival, and the courtyard of the Jui Tui Temple is crowded with palanquins containing the gods, borne on the shoulders of groups of youths dressed entirely in white. Suddenly a man, his face impaled with a rod, body gleaming with sweat, marches into the temple. Temple elders apply to his cheeks a large piece of gold foil soaked in a concoction containing coconut oil, and slowly withdraw the rod; there is almost no bleeding. Immediately, the man approaches the altar, slaps his palms on the top of it and shouts 'Bai!' – an ancient Chinese word, the meaning of which no one, least of all the devotee himself, apparently understands. Other elders frenetically beat the temple drums and bang cymbals; the noise is cacophonous. The man's head begins to shake, his mouth foams, his body convulses, his eyes roll into the back of his head – he is possessed by the gods, but the evil spirits have withdrawn from his body. He then faints and falls limply into the arms of the elders. For some moments, it appears as if his heart has physically stopped; there is not the slightest movement from him. Then the temple elders begin to slap his face and slowly, very slowly, his eyes start to open, although he seems to be in a total daze, confused and unaware of his surroundings. This banishment ritual is repeated time after time throughout the day, with hundreds of devotees entering the temple to rid themselves of the spirits. In all cases there was virtually no bleeding or scarring from the body piercing, however extreme, and those that put themselves through these rituals believe that in so doing they act as mediums for the gods.

On the evening of the last day of the Song Dao, after a further parade through the town to the deafening accompaniment of yet more firecrackers, Phuket's temples disgorge their elders and the faithful, who march to the ocean for the final element of the festival. They carry with them the sacred urn of the Kiu Ong Iah. At midnight, to chanting prayers, they bid farewell to the visiting gods by solemnly dispersing the ashes from the urn into the sea. As the ashes are washed away by the tide, the Nine Emperor Gods begin their ascent to heaven, having cleansed and purified Phuket for another year.

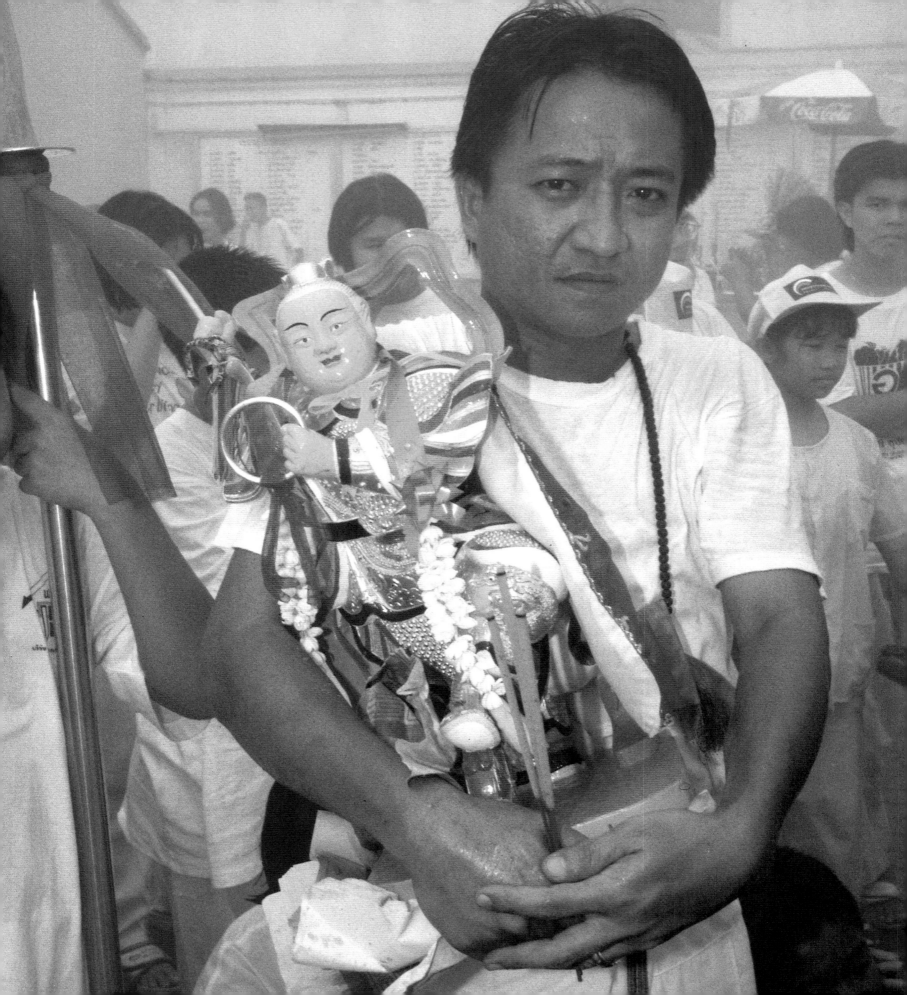

The rain was torrential that day. Nyaung Shwe, gateway to Inle Lake, was flooded and the villagers were wading through water waist high – none of them could remember a time when the roads through their village had been so inundated. 'All due to global warming,' they said, for this was supposedly the dry season. On the few sections of roads above the flood waters, bicyclists pedalled laboriously, holding umbrellas above their heads, while the only other form of transport still operating were the wiry ponies pulling four-seater traps fitted with a roof and quaint side curtains. During a lull in the rain squalls we clambered aboard a long, slender *canu* and motored south down a narrow canal, our baggage tied down in the bow. We passed an occasional *canu* much smaller than ours, laden down to the water-line with ripening tomatoes, and paddled one-legged from the stern. The bizarre rowing style of the villagers has evolved from their aquatic lifestyle. The majority earn their living either by fishing or from cultivating flowers and vegetables on 'floating' gardens made from a combination of lake weed, mud and water hyacinths tethered to the lake floor by bamboo stakes, and using just one leg as propulsion for the *canu* frees their hands and arms for netting fish or tending their floating agricultural produce.

Rudyard Kipling, in his *Letters from the East* (1898), wrote: 'This is Burma, and it will be quite unlike any other land you knew about.' And he was right, for at the end of the channel we suddenly entered a lake quite dazzling in its brilliance, framed by mountains to left and right and with great swathes of rolling clouds reflected in its gleaming waters. And the sun came out.

Inle Lake is the home of the indigenous Intha (the 'sons of the lake') who are believed to have migrated here from south-east Burma at the end of the fourteenth century. Today, 80,000 of them live in around sixty-four floating villages scattered across the lake. Wherever I looked, there were *paya* peppering the landscape, their golden roofs glistening in the now brilliant sunshine. There are probably a thousand of these pagoda-like temples around the lake and a further hundred inhabited *kyaung* (monasteries), twenty-three of which participate in the festival of Phaung Daw U. The festival takes place over eighteen days during the period of the full moon of Thadingyut, which falls between September and November. Although the celebrations have apparently been taking place for centuries no one seemed to know quite when they began. Our young guide, Toe Aung Than, who knew about every other aspect of the lake and its people, was only able to tell me that 'the schedule has been passed down from generation to generation'.

The objects of the Intha people's veneration are five stumpy statues which reside in the Phaung Daw U *paya*, one of the three most sacred shrines in Burma. Three of these are said to be of the Buddha, the other two of disciples; they are thought to have been carved from sandalwood and donated to the twelfth-century Burmese King Alaungsithu by the *nat* spirit gods. For centuries, worshippers have been affixing squares of gold leaf to them and the build-up of gold is such that

any discernible carving on them has completely disappeared. The festival provides an opportunity for all the 'sons of the lake' to pay homage to these images, which are transported daily to a different *kyaung* by an enormous golden *karaweik*, a copy of an ancient Burmese ceremonial royal barge carved in the shape of a swan. Some years ago the *karaweik* capsized in the middle of the lake and only four of the images were saved. On returning these to the *paya*, however, the distressed villagers were astonished to find the fifth already there on its pedestal – covered in weed. Since this miracle, the fifth statue always remains at the *paya*, acting as a 'guardian' during the annual lake perigrinations. A tall pillar surmounted by the head of a golden swan, *shwe hintha*, marks the spot where the potential catastrophe took place.

The *karaweik* moves from *kyaung* to *kyaung* behind a huge waterborne procession. First come the slender and immensely long *hley*, leg-rowed by some forty-six oarsmen. These vessels in turn pull a further series of *hley* carrying female dancers and singers whose incantations herald the arrival of a duo of *karaweik*, the smaller one acting as a kind of consort to the principal *karaweik*. Taking up the final position astern comes the great *karaweik*, covered from bow to stern in gold leaf and carrying the four sacred statues under an awning of white umbrellas.

The *karaweik* docks at every major *kyaung* for sufficient time to enable all the monks and villagers there to bring offerings of food as homage to the golden images. The beautiful wooden Nga-phe-*kyaung*, for instance, is noted not only as a fine example of nineteenth-century teak-framed construction but also because it has a large cat population who have been trained by the monks to jump through hoops – it's often now referred to as The Jumping Cat Monastery.

The journeys of the *karaweik* entourage were colourful and serenely beautiful, but the celebrations on the final day, outside the Phaung Daw U *paya*, outshone all previous sights. By dawn, hundreds of *canu*, crammed with multi-hued turbanned villagers, were already moored in prime positions – 'The colours of the hill-tribes who attend the festival,' wrote Sir George Scott in the nineteenth century, 'are like wind-stirred tulip beds'. A constant criss-cross of boats deposited monks at the jetty of the *paya* or jostled for position, and stalls were selling every imaginable religious accoutrement, including small squares of gold-leaf for 100 kyat (6 cents) that would be affixed to the four images after their final journey home. You could sense in the air the growing excitement at the return of the four statues to the *paya* for another twelve months.

And then the long-awaited moment. A *hley* bearing thirty crimson-costumed *kachathe* dancers was the first boat to hove into view, followed by an even longer *hley*, rowed by some fifty or so women garlanded in pink, their green-tipped oars sending up a fine spray as their blades stroked the surface of the water. And then the golden swan-shaped prow of the *karaweik* appeared, towed by a fleet of the longest *hley* I'd ever seen, each rowed by about a hundred *hley hlew the ma* oarsmen. To the cacophonous sound of xylophones and drums the *karaweik* slowly eased into position beside the dock of the *paya*; it had brought its sacred cargo safely home again.

In describing these outrageously beautiful scenes, I am not unmindful of the controversial issues of a country governed by a dictatorial and repressive military regime, but I was also conscious that the ceremonies were an echo of the pomp and splendour I was told was once typical of Burmese royal life in centuries past.

**page 202–203**  Much of Inle Lake is covered with 'floating gardens'. A long *hley* being rowed through one of the many narrow canal creates a mirage-like image as it floats past a lagoon of waterlilies.

**page 205**  On each of the eighteen days of the festival, as the *karaweik* transports the sacred images to another monastery on the lake, it is preceded by spectacular processions.

**page 206–207**  Tall grasses waving gently in the wind appear to mimic the grace and fluidity of the *kachathe* dancers.

**page 209**  top  In order to be in a prime position, the villagers each day would always anchor their *canu* hours in advance of the arrival of the golden *karaweik*.

**page 209**  bottom  The lake's sacred statues are now wholly unrecognisable as Buddhist images, as for centuries the 'sons of the lake' have paid homage by covering them with countless squares of gold leaf. They also rub small red or yellow cloths over them, which they keep as a talisman until the next festival.

**page 210**  top  I lodged in a cottage built on stilts in the middle of the lake, and while sitting on the balcony early on the last morning of the festival, I saw this *hley* drifting slowly by on its way towards the *paya*.

**page 210**  bottom  The rowing style of the Intha people is unique. They 'leg-row' by wrapping one leg around the oar and power their *hley* forward, often at considerable speed, with the legs only; their arms are merely used to help balance the oar.

**page 212–213**  The climax to the festival: the *karaweik* with its sacred cargo journeys back to the Phaung Daw U *paya*.

When I was researching prior to visiting Bali for this festival, the unstable political situation on the Indonesian island of East Timor had not been resolved and I needed to know whether the problems there were likely to spread to Bali and coincide with the celebrations. I soon discovered that the Balinese do not consider their island to be part of Indonesia – Bali belongs to the gods!

Although the Balinese are Hindu, the religion that they practise is very different from the Indian variety and reflects the island's colourful history – a blend of Hindu, Buddhist, Javanese and ancient indigenous beliefs. They worship Brahma, Ganesh, Shiva and Vishnu, but the majority of shrines are dedicated to gods and spirits that are uniquely Balinese. They believe strongly in magic and the power of spirits and much of their religion is based on this. In Balinese belief the good spirits inhabit the mountains while the ogres and demons live in the sea.

Bali is a relatively small island – it's only about 130 kilometres long and 80 kilometres wide – but it is home to an estimated hundred thousand temples, and you encounter them everywhere, from the jungle-clad mountain tops to the palm-fringed beaches. Every village has at least three. The *pura puseh*, the 'temple of origin', faces the mountains and is dedicated to the founders of the village. Then the *pura desa* is normally situated in the centre of the village and dedicated to the welfare of the inhabitants, while the third, the *pura dalem*, faces the sea and is dedicated to the spirits of the dead. Almost every house also has its own shrine and most villages have many other monuments, too, to the spirits of agriculture and art. Bali has several religious sites of great importance, notably Pura Besakih, a huge complex of sixty temples nestling in the clouds on the slopes of Gunung Agung. This sacred volcano, rising up 3140 metres, is known as 'the navel of the world'.

Offerings play a very significant role in Balinese life as these are thought to pacify the gods and therefore bring good health and prosperity to each family. Each day believers place *canang sari*, little trays containing symbolic food, flowers and money, in temples, on shrines, outside houses and even at dangerous crossroads.

The Balinese have celebrations for every facet of daily life – births, weddings, teeth-pulling, rice-planting and rain-stopping – and of course to honour the gods. The Government Tourist Board publishes an annual calendar highlighting every temple festival and holy day throughout the island, and these number at least two hundred – a month. Identifying the exact time and location can be very complicated because the islanders follow not only the twelve-month lunar calendar but also a separate *wuku* calendar of 210 days, effectively celebrating the New Year every seven months. I had come to Bali for the great holiday of Galungan-Kuningan. The first five days celebrate the victory of Virtue, Dharma, over Evil, Adharma, before the day of Galungan, when the ancestral spirits come down to earth to live in the homes of their descendants. The second part is the Feast of All Souls, ten days later, when these ancestral spirits and gods return to their home in heaven.

**page 214–215** There are an estimated hundred thousand temples on Bali and at almost every one of these a celebration takes place during the ten days of this Galungan-Kuningan. This temple is high up on the sacred volcano of Gunung Agung.

**page 217** Women bringing symbolic offerings of food and flowers to one of the many temples on Gunung Agung appear as splashes of muted colour against the thick cloud that envelops the upper slopes of this active volcano.

**page 218–219** Each temple is surrounded by *penjor* – tall, gaily decorated bamboo poles. The higher the *penjor,* the greater the chance that the gods can see them from where they reside.

**page 220** Balinese women have perfected the art of creating *pabanten*, the exquisitely arranged pyramids of food that they present to the gods.

**page 221** At each of the island's largest temples a *gamelan* orchestra plays throughout the ceremonies. An orchestra may comprise up to forty players.

**page 221** The *wahi* is danced for the gods, not for an audience, and I was extremely fortunate to see these dancers, wreathed in clouds of incense, performing in the inner courtyard of their village temple.

**page 222** These village girls hold their hands up in prayer as the *pemangku*, the village priest, sprinkles them with holy water.

The prelude to this festival is the cockfighting in the village temples. This is an essential part of the celebrations because the villagers believe that the land is revived by the drawing of blood. At each contest, there's much yelling and shouting as bets are taken, then a gong sounds to start the fight. The cocks are equipped with long steel blades attached to their right feet and the birds attack each other so furiously that bouts are frequently over in less than a minute. It's easy to be shocked at the brutality, but the Balinese look on these bloody fights quite differently. To them a cock is as dead whether it has been killed in the ring or with a hatchet in the kitchen. Either way it provides food for the festive banquet, and dying in a Galungan cockfight makes it a religious offering.

During Galungan the entire island is adorned with *penjor*, tall, elaborately decorated bamboo poles which are erected outside the entrance to every house. The *penjor* symbolize prosperity, and their height is determined by the belief that the gods can see them from the tops of the mountains where they dwell. Throughout the days of celebration, *barongs* appear prancing along the roads. These strange, lion-like monsters are almost life-size, masked and ornamented and bedecked with enormous fleeces of long human hair. Each is carried by two men. These mythical 'lions' are treated with great respect and addressed by titles such as Lord of the Jungle or The Big One, for they are considered to represent the sun, the light, medicine and, most importantly, represent the antithesis of evil.

At each temple, the women bring *pabanten*, offerings for the gods of very tall, exquisitely arranged pyramids of food, fruit, cakes and flowers. All these offerings must be beautifully made and presented to please the gods, but the Balinese consider the actual giving of food to be a form of tax. In 'paying' it, they are able to give back something that rightly belongs to the spirits.

From the forecourt of each temple come the curious harmonies of the gamelan angklung. This is a portable band comprising about six tuned gongs and metallophones. Lines of male elders sit along the walls of the *djaban*, the outer courtyard of the temple, holding long spears and wearing embroidered yellow sarongs. Meanwhile, behind the wall of the *dalam*, the temple's inner courtyard, and wreathed in clouds of burning incense, are the young women of the village. Dressed in the brightest embroidered silks, emblazoned with yellow sashes, and with their hair garlanded with golden frangipani flowers, they perform the sacred *wahi* dance to the sound of spiritual incantations.

Almost every village has its own daily celebration during Galungan-Kuningan, usually at dusk when the air is cooler. Some are formal temple rituals, but others might take place spontaneously on the street. One evening I watched about a hundred villagers sit down in the middle of their main road, blocking all traffic. To the accompaniment of drums and bamboo instruments, they formed a semi-circle and sat on their haunches, barefoot, awaiting the day's spectacle. First a *pemangku*, or village priest, blessed the 'arena' formed by the villagers by sprinkling holy water among them, and then young female *pendet* dancers, their hair tied back with bandannas of flowers, and attired in sarongs sumptuously woven with gold thread, performed their welcome dance in honour of the gods. Finally, as more incense was wafted across the villagers, and the drums were beaten more stridently, the *pemangku* suddenly drew out from a raffia basket by his side three pullets which he swiftly decapitated with his bare hands, throwing the headless bodies into the crowd. It was wholly unexpected and for a moment the villagers were entranced and transfixed by the sacrifice.

'Lord Brahma was worried over the matter of not having a place in his name on earth as other Gods have…Having such thoughts in mind and after saying "Managal Ho" he threw a lotus flower upon the earth. The flower fell at three places and the holy water sprang out from all these three places. Then Lord Brahma said that these places would be known as Pushkar…And further he added that these three *kunds* [lakes] would be famous for removing the sins of sinners. As Brahmaji threw the *pushpa* [flower] with his *kar* [hand], so he gave the name of Pushkar to this place.'.

So Mohan Lal Goyal explains the origins of Pushkar in the official guidebook to the town: *A Place of Lord Brahma – the Holiest Place of the Hindus.*

Pushkar lies just north-west of the seventh-century city of Ajmer in Rajasthan and is approached by a scenic, winding road that cuts through the Nag Pahar, Snake Mountain. Known as 'the dwelling place of all the gods', Pushkar has been a pilgrimage destination since the fourth century AD, and although the precise date of its origin is unknown, according to the official guide, there are references to it 'in the oldest religious books of the Hindus'.

Bathing at any of the *tirthas*, India's holy places, washes away sins, but only the lake at Pushkar – the most sacred in all India – and a *darshan* (an audience with a guru) 'makes a sinner free from all the deadliest sins; to die at this place is salvation giving'. The most auspicious time to bathe here is the time of the full moon and, for maximum benefit, during Kartika Purnima, the five days preceding the full moon in November, for Lord Brahma declared that 'during these five days, all the gods will remain present at Pushkar and bless the people.'

For these five days, a gigantic *mela* (fair) sets up in the lakeside town to feed, equip and entertain the hundreds of thousands who attend the bathing ceremonies. During my visit there was a ferris wheel, a circus, 'the Great Mayani Magician', and go-go dancers in bikini tops, their teeth and mouths stained bright red by the endless chewing of betel leaves. Stalls sold mountains of quilts, blankets, rugs, shawls, staves, axes, cooking utensils and holy potions, and there were avenues of camel and horse saddles, belts, bridles and beads for decorating the animals. There were puppet shows and hypnotists and stalls where you could try your luck at 'Gam of Sikl' [sic]. Archaic 8mm equipment projected old BBC wildlife documentaries without the sound and an unmanned tractor turning endless circles was watched by transfixed villagers. A *mela* magistrate and court sat to resolve any dissension or squabbles in the tens of thousands of transactions being conducted day and night.

Around the perimeter of this bustling commercial area, in the sand dunes of the desert, was a further market, this one of livestock: bullocks, sheep, horses, goats and camels – thousands of camels, tethered or hobbled, as far as you could see. Of all the camels in India, 85 per cent are in Rajasthan, and most of them seemed to be in Pushkar. You could trade camels for breeding, for

racing, for riding or just for pulling the cart that is the staple transport of the region. Around 7000 rupees would buy an adult camel, or you could hire one for 30 rupees a day. At dusk, the women and children would collect camel dung to fuel the fires around which the camel owners would crouch as they cooked their evening meal.

Judging by the volume of trade, it might have seemed that secular activities had taken over the religious nature of the gathering. But there would be no *mela* without the holy men and the thousands of pilgrims who journey by train, truck, camel cart or on foot to bathe in the lake and 'do *puja*', acts of worship. Two brothers I met had ridden by camel from the desert town of Jaisalmer in just six days – a distance of over 400 kilometres.

The lake at Pushkar is surrounded by 52 *ghats*, bathing areas approached by steep stone stairways. They were constructed by different kings and emperors over the years; some have more religious importance than others. I walked through the town and down to the lake, past throngs of villagers haggling at yet more stalls, to see pilgrims descending to the *ghats* in a continuous stream, both men and women removing all but a loincloth before entering the water. During the five days of Kartika, pilgrims take their daily dip either in the early morning or at dusk, but the most auspicious hour this year was to be between four and five in the morning of the day of the full moon itself, the final day of the *mela*.

The preceding day, more and yet more pilgrims arrived; the local paper estimated that two or three *lakh* (a *lakh* is a hundred thousand) entered the town on that day alone. At dusk the cacophony was deafening, an endless chanting and jangling of bells melding into a continuous blur of sound that rose to a crescendo at dawn. In counterpoint came the rasping gurgle of camels out on the dunes, being saddled up for their day's work.

At first light I walked down to the lake and was immediately ensnared in the torrent of humankind forcing its way to the *ghats*. I passed *sadhus* (holy men) sitting cross-legged in doorways, an apparition of Hanuman, the monkey-god, misshapen freaks, mutant bullocks, and, among other grotesques, a seemingly lifeless torso covered in white ash and painted with pink spots, with a feeding bowl beside him into which pilgrims were depositing nuts and berries. A one-way system was supposedly in operation but was failing to work. Near one of the principal *ghats*, the crush built up to a point where disaster seemed inevitable, but the pilgrims rapidly became orderly and well-behaved and the river of humanity began safely flowing again towards the water.

At the lakeside, the *ghats* were crammed with devotees washing themselves, while those who could swim were further out, doing *puja* by bobbing up and down as ducks do in a pond. Holy men at the top of the stairways offered pilgrims, for a rupee or two, a brief mantra to complete the process of purification, and held out small bowls of the powders required to replace the *tilak* mark on the forehead that had been washed away in the lake.

By midday, the tide of pilgrims had ebbed. Several hundred camels were still hobbled in the dunes but the thousands of the previous day had disappeared back across the desert. The ferris wheel was still revolving, the go-go dancers still gyrating in front of a dwindling yet still enraptured audience, and the *mela* police reported that just three pilgrims had drowned in the lake. The Pushkar Mela was over until the next Kartika Purnima.

**page 224–225** A film director would be hard pressed to improve upon this 'set piece' that I came upon down at the lakeside in the early morning.

**page 227** Sitting beside a *ghat*, a *sadhu* or holy man waits to administer to pilgrims who wish to have a *darshan* with him, thereby becoming cleansed of all the deadly sins.

**page 229** top Rajasthani women have an innate sense of style and colour, and a major celebration is an opportunity for them to wear their finest jewellery and decorations.

**page 229** bottom This group of entertainers by the side of the road were on their way to the huge Pushkar camel fair that runs in parallel to the spiritual Kartika Purnima celebration.

**page 230–231** All over the *mela* ground during the late afternoon, young Rajasthani women can be found dancing, and large crowds gather to watch the spontaneous entertainment.

**page 232** Professional dance troupes of eunuchs spend the year travelling from fair to fair.

**page 233** I saw this human personification of the monkey-god Hanuman in an alley off one of the *ghats*. Hanuman represents selfless dedication.

**page 234** Even though Pushkar is one of India's most holy places, the camel fair that is held concurrently with the sacred ceremonies is the largest in India and thousands of camels are traded here during the period of Kartika Purmina.

**page 235** As dusk falls these camel dealers are preparing for a night in the desert with their herd.

**page 236–237** This is not a still from a Hollywood epic: images like this can be seen every night during the Pushkar celebrations.

guadalupe, sierra tarahumara

Families had been arriving in the little square of the *ranchería* throughout the day. With their thick woollen blankets over the shoulders and carrying their spears and staves, they sat quietly on the ground, enjoying the warmth of the sun and preparing for what was going to be a long day and night of drinking and celebration.

It was 12 December, the day of Our Lady of Guadalupe. Nuestra Señora de Guadalupe is a manifestation of the Virgin Mary who appeared to a Mexican Indian, Juan Diego, in 1531. She is the patron saint of Mexico, and her feast day is fêted all over the country. I was fortunate enough to have been invited by the Instituto Nacional Indigenista – a kind of bureau of Indian affairs – to spend some weeks among the Tarahumara, and at the time of the *fiesta* was 2750 metres up in the Sierra Tarahumara, in the remote pueblo of Norogachi.

The Tarahumara live in an extraordinary time capsule. To the Mestizos – Mexicans of mixed Spanish and Indian blood – the Tarahumara are *cimarrones* or wild animals, while they call themselves Rarámuri, footrunners, in their Uto-Aztecan language. Their ancestors probably came across the Bering Strait from Asia about twenty thousand years ago and they've lived in the Sierra Madre of western Chihuahua for perhaps two thousand years. There are probably fewer than fifty thousand of them today, inhabiting mountainous country riven by magnificent *barrancas* or canyons, some of which are more than 1500 metres deep. It is this isolated, inhospitable environment that has enabled them to preserve their lifestyle virtually unchanged. I had been told that the Tarahumara were reluctant to talk about themselves, particularly as few of the adults understand Spanish. As a result, apparently bizarre tales have evolved about them, describing them as a race of mysterious cave-dwellers, as the sentinels of long-lost gold and silver mines, as runners of superhuman ability.

The topography of the region means that many do live in caves, particularly in the winter. And in this vertiginous, largely roadless territory even horses, although prestigious to own, have no value as a mode of transport, so a Tarahumara tends to run – often considerable distances.

Every young Tarahumara wants to become a great runner. Herding goats and sheep on the cliffs gives him ample exercise from childhood, but what he trains for is *rarájipari* – the kick-ball race. This is usually run during the warm summer nights over a distance that can be as much as 200 kilometres. The circuit is lit by pitch-pine torches and betting is intense, particularly by the runners themselves. The game is played by two teams, each of which aim to get their ball across the finish line first. It mustn't be touched by hand, so the runners pass it to each other, football style. The technique involves lifting the ball slightly with the toes (particularly necessary in crossing streams), and I asked some young children if they'd show me. But apparently a demonstration was insufficient; it had to be a competitive race. The two teams of six-year-olds soon disappeared down a steep track, returning about half an hour later, having run about seven kilometres!

**page 238–239** These girls were walking down from the high sierra to attend the evening celebrations in Norogachi. Their winter clothing comprises a headband for binding their hair, a loose blouse, a sash holding up their wide skirts, called *sipucaka*, and a thick blanket thrown over their shoulders.

**page 240** Music plays an essential part in a *tesgüinada*, and all the instruments are manufactured by the Indians themselves. This couple were waiting at the side of the road for a truck to take them on to a *ranchería*.

**page 242–243** *Matachines* performing outside the church at Norogachi. Over their everyday dress they wear a cape that hangs down to their knees, and on their heads a *corona* made of bark. Coloured stockings and boots complete their home-made festive wardrobe – this is one of the few occasions when a Tarahumara wears anything on his feet other than sandals made from old rubber truck tyres.

**page 244** top The *matachines* will dance non-stop for at least an hour, beating time with their rattles while the accompanying vio-linists play a repetitive series of musical phrases.

**page 244** bottom The Tarahumara have utilised stringed instru-ments since the middle of the eighteenth century, and these crude yet effective violins are played at the majority of fiestas.

**page 247** top Norogachi is the centre of one of the oldest Jesuit missionaries in Mexico. During the period of La Fiesta de Nuestra Señora de Guadalupe, food, drink and plants are all 'offered' before the cross in the square outside the church.

**page 247** bottom At an altitude of about 3000 metres, December nights can get extremely cold. Many of the Tarahumara women and children shelter in the church during the night of Guadalupe while the *matachines* continue their dances inside it.

The Tarahumara life is a simple one: they produce most of what they need and, as they barter their produce against other requirements, have little need for money. The Jesuit Padre Joseph Neuman, who lived among them for fifty years from 1681, described them as:

'simple of nature, and unpolished; swarthy of colour but not black; of good height and solidly made, but extremely unwilling to work. They always go armed with bows and arrows, and these are their only weapons. Their arrows are envenomed with a deadly poison…and they are much feared by other tribes…they show rather a lazy indifference to everything good, unlimited sensual desire, an irresistible habit of getting drunk…'

The bow has largely been replaced by the throwing stick and the axe, but mass drunkenness at drinking parties called *tesgüinadas* is still the most important thing in a Tarahumara's life. Four hundred years ago, the Jesuit missionaries disapproved of their beer cult, yet drinking *tesgüino*, beer made from fermented corn, is still at the very core of social and economic life. Even to begin to fathom the Tarahumara, I was told, I had to try to understand their need for these drinking parties, which were fundamental to the way they lived – and celebrated. It was therefore essential to participate in a *tesgüinada*.

My Spanish-speaking Tarahumara guide, José-Maria, took me to the rancho – a group of about twenty families – of Caborachi. As we walked towards an isolated cluster of crudely constructed shacks I was first aware that a *tesgüinada* was in progress by the number of bodies sprawled across the track. A couple were snoring heavily, a young baby feeding at its dormant mother's breast. And then the stillness of the plateau was shattered by music coming from a tiny timber dwelling. Inside, about twenty people were passing around gourds filled with *tesgüino* which had been made in a large black clay *olla*. An accordionist was accompanied by a violinist, both of them stopping every minute or so to take another gulp of beer. More musicians played outside as couples danced closely together. One of them staggered up to me, talking rapidly in Tarahumara, and offered me a gourdful of *tesgüino*. It bore no relationship to any beer I had ever drunk, being greeny yellow, slightly sweet and glutinous, but it was refreshingly cold and intoxicating.

*Tesgüino* is made by fermenting sprouting corn with a grass seed called *basiahuari*. The process takes about seven days, but the beer can only be drunk during a limited 24-hour period. A Tarahumara uses at least 90 kilos of corn a year in the production of *tesgüino*, sufficient to provide a family of four with food for a month. Although the Jesuit priests deny it, each adult attends – at the very minimum – fifty *tesgüinadas* a year. Etiquette requires everyone at a *tesgüinada* to drink as much as possible (although drinking *esquiate*, a kind of mushed cornmeal, beforehand, diminishes the effects somewhat).

The Tarahumara have an amazing capacity for beer, yet are not alcoholics. Drinking is essentially a social event at which business discussions can take place, marriages arranged or wife-swapping organized. In fact, after a drinking session the first questions that a Tarahumara will ask are: 'What did you dream? Where did you sleep? How many times did you do it last night?' The only time that a young unmarried Tarahumara can 'get it together' is likely to be after a *tesgüinada*.

*Tesgüino* is also used as payment. When someone wants help with weeding, harvesting or building a corral, he invites his neighbours from the surrounding *rancherías* to assist him, and in return

page 248 The first rays of the sun break over the sierra as the *matachines* continue their rhythmic rattling. They have already been dancing continuously for about eight hours.

page 249 The morning after the *fiesta*, a Tarahumara, enveloped in a thick woollen blanket, stands in the early morning sunshine to get some warmth and recover from the night's festivities.

page 250-251 I attended this *tesgüinada* in a *rancheria* about a week before the main *fiesta*. It's both an opportunity for neighbours to socialize and for the fields, crops and animals to be 'cured'. A Tarahumara will attend on average about fifty *tesgüinadas* annually. Someone will play a guitar, a violin or an accordion and everyone participates in the dancing; the alcohol consumed breaks down the Tarahumara's inherent isolated existence and creates a sense of a group spirit.

provides them with beer. The obligation of giving *tesgüinadas* can often cause extreme hardship, for a Tarahumara who has little corn must from necessity use the majority for beer-making.

A Tarahumara's wealth is gauged by the number of sheep, cattle and goats he owns. He rarely eats them other than at sacrificial feasts after a *fiesta*, but their manure is invaluable as fertilizer. The method of fertilization in highly ingenious. He builds a wooden corral about 6 metres in diameter and pens in the animals at night. After about five nights, he asks his neighbours to help him move the corral – in return for a *tesgüinada*. Soon he has fertilized a large enough area of barren, rocky land to cultivate enough corn for *tesgüino* and *pinole*, a nutritious flour produced from roasted kernels, for his needs. And that ground will be sufficiently enriched to last for a further four years of planting. A wealthier man will often lend his stock to his less well-off relatives, but there are still millions of hectares that remain fallow because of insufficient domestic animals to fertilize it.

The Tarahumara have an affinity with animals, and believe that they're not only intelligent but that they talk a language which they don't understand. They are therefore reluctant to kill any animal that does not harm either themselves or the corn. I was told that they will eat almost anything that walks or crawls, even lice; and included in their diet are grasshoppers and caterpillars, frogs, lizards and rattlesnakes, the dried blood from cattle as well as small wild mammals from rats and mice (considered a particular delicacy) to raccoons and peccaries.

In Norogachi, where one of the earliest missionaries was founded, I met Padre Jesus Hielo, at the time the Jesuits' only Tarahumara priest. I asked him to describe his people. After a lengthy pause, his reply was brief but exactly expressed their philosophy: 'Their subjective attitude towards Nature makes them feel at one with their Creator. They respect Nature above all else, believing that all their daily requirements are derived from Mother Earth. They need to ask Her for a fertile harvest and if She is not "looked after" She'll take revenge by sending drought, flood or lightning, or worms to eat the corn.'

Virtually all Tarahumaras today are *bautizados* – baptized ones – but a central figure in Tarahumara culture remains the shaman. One of a shaman's most important functions is the 'curing' of fields and animals each year. Father Luis Verplancken, who had lived in the Sierra Tarahumara for thirty years, described their role: 'They talk to the cows, they guide the baby calves to fresh pastures and make sure that they come back to the corral every night. They talk to the plants, saying: "Please grow big and give fat kernels and make sure that the worms don't eat you."' The worms, which attack the roots of the corn, mustn't be harmed as if they get angry they might ruin the crop.

Christianized Tarahumara apparently consider the Jesuits to be 'hot-shot bewitchers with a direct line to God'. The padre told me that at one festival, 'the Indians got drunk and the priest arrived and was furious. The following year, they had no rain. They believed that the priest had talked to God asking Him not to send any rain.'

This, then, was the background to the primitive *fiesta* of Nuestra Señora de Guadalupe among the Tarahumara.

The key participants were the musicians – the fiddlers, guitar players and drummers – and the *matachines*, the dancers. The fiddlers settled themselves on the terrace outside the church and proved capable of playing for hours on end, quite hypnotically, while the *matachines* danced to the

frenzied tattoo of their rattles. There were about twenty-five of them, dressed in tunics and *coronas* or crowns of mirrors, led by the *monarco* – the monarch.

Late into the night, all the inhabitants of the pueblo, who had been seated around roaring bonfires drinking prodigious quantities of *tesgüino*, now assembled in the square and began packing into the church, many with their animals. The monotonous music continued outside but then, as if on a signal, the fiddlers stopped playing and the rattles were abandoned. In the eerie silence the *matachines* danced on, the only sound now the slightly macabre jangling of their crowns.

This extraordinary silent dancing carried on through the night until, at about 4.a.m, they retired into the church and collapsed into a deep sleep on the floor. As the first rays of dawn began to stretch like jet trails across the eastern sky, the musicians once again began to play, accompanied by pounding drums. The *matachines* managed to draw themselves from their sleep to recommence their frantic rattling in the middle of the square. It was now apparent, however, that only those with the strongest alcoholic constitutions remained on their feet, the remainder having succumbed to the effects of this long, drawn-out beer party. Father Verplancken later commented: 'They are not slaves of time or civilization. They have mastered how to survive in this land for centuries with the very minimum from the outside world. Destroying their culture will destroy them as a race.'

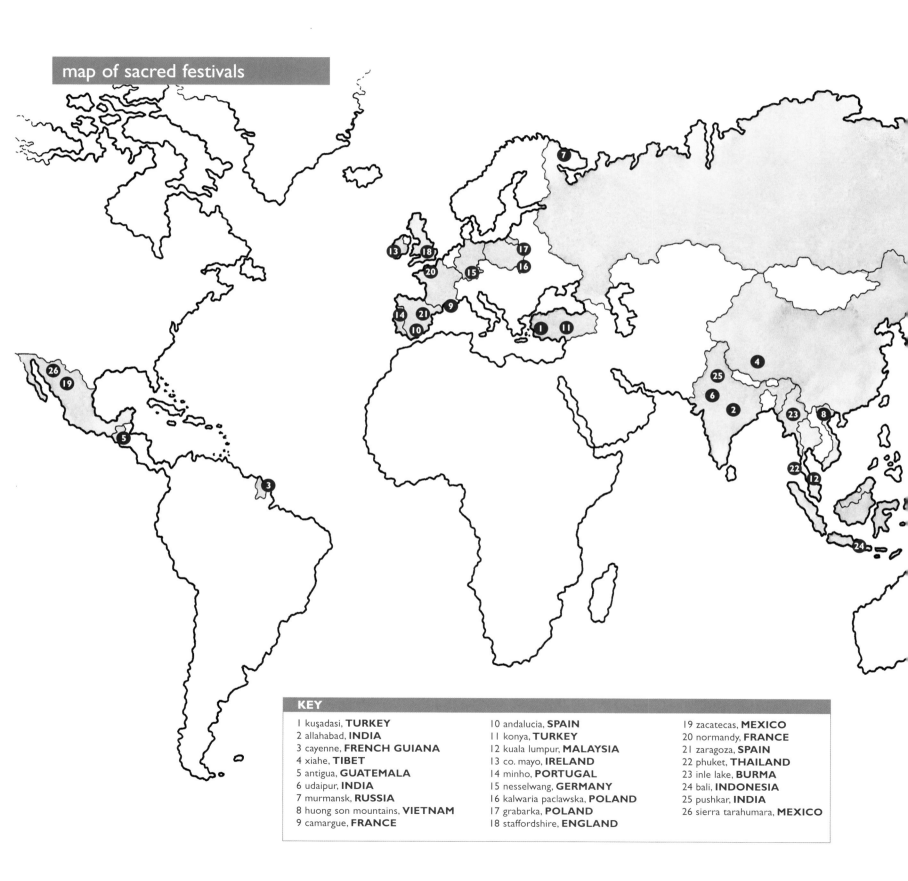

## map of sacred festivals

### KEY

1 kuşadasi, **TURKEY**
2 allahabad, **INDIA**
3 cayenne, **FRENCH GUIANA**
4 xiahe, **TIBET**
5 antigua, **GUATEMALA**
6 udaipur, **INDIA**
7 murmansk, **RUSSIA**
8 huong son mountains, **VIETNAM**
9 camargue, **FRANCE**

10 andalucia, **SPAIN**
11 konya, **TURKEY**
12 kuala lumpur, **MALAYSIA**
13 co. mayo, **IRELAND**
14 minho, **PORTUGAL**
15 nesselwang, **GERMANY**
16 kalwaria paclawska, **POLAND**
17 grabarka, **POLAND**
18 staffordshire, **ENGLAND**

19 zacatecas, **MEXICO**
20 normandy, **FRANCE**
21 zaragoza, **SPAIN**
22 phuket, **THAILAND**
23 inle lake, **BURMA**
24 bali, **INDONESIA**
25 pushkar, **INDIA**
26 sierra tarahumara, **MEXICO**

# bibliography

GENERAL

Dates and Meanings of Religious and Other Festivals, Dr John Walshe, *W. Foulsham and Co., London, 1989*

Dictionary of Festivals, J.C. Cooper, *Thorsons, London, 1995*

Faith, Mike Abrahams, *Network, London, 2000*

Faiths and Festivals, Martin Palmer, *Ward Lock, London, 1984*

Festivals and Celebrations, Rowland Purton, Basil Blackwell, *Oxford, 1989*

Festivals in World Religions, edited by Adam Brown, *Shap, 1986*

Festivals in World Religions, Peter Woodward, *The Shap Working Party on World Religions in Education, RMEP, 1998*

Hard Travel to Sacred Places, Rudolph Wurlitzer, *Shambhala, Boston, 1995*

On Pilgrimage, Jini Fiennes, *Sinclair-Stevenson, London, 1991*

Pilgrimage, Siam, *J.W. Northend, Sheffield, 2000*

Ritual, *Magnum/André Deutsch, London, 1990*

Sacred Dance – Encounters with the Gods, Maria-Gabriele Wosien, *Thames and Hudson, London, 1989*

Shaman – the Wonder Healer, Joan Halifax, *Thames and Hudson, London, 1990*

The Spiritual Tourist, Mick Brown, *Bloomsbury, London, 1999*

BALI

Island of Bali, Miguel Covarrubias, *Periplus, Jakarta, Indonesia 1973*

FRANCE

Les-Saintes-Maries de-la-Mer, Camargue, Alain Albaric, *Editions Vent Large, Paris, 1998*

Mont-Saint-Michel, Lucien Bély, *Editions Ouest-France, Rennes, 1999*

Mont-Saint-Michel, Marc Déceneux, *Editions Ouest-France, Rennes, 1995*

Mont-Saint-Michel, A Sacred and Symbolic History, Marc Déceneux, *Editions Ouest-France, Rennes, 1996*

GUATEMALA

Guatemalan Guide, Peter Glassman, *Passport Press, New York, 1987*

INDIA

Fairs and Festivals of Rajasthan, *Department of Tourism, Arts and Culture, Government of Rajasthan, Jaipur, 1999*

Festivals of India, *National Book Trust, India, 1982*

Festivals of India, Asharani Mathur and Rupinder Khullar, *India Book Distributors, Bombay, 1995*

Hindu Feasts, Fasts and Ceremonies, *Srishti Publishers and Distributors, New Delhi, 1999*

Hindu Gods and Goddesses, Ashish Khokar, *Rupa and Co, New Delhi, 1993*

Pushkar, the Holiest Place of the Hindus, Mohan Lal Goyal, *Bhakti Gyan Mandir, Ajmer, 1987*

Religions of India, Dr Karan Singh, *Clarion Books, New Delhi, 1983*

Sadhus – Holy Men of India, Dolf Hartsuiker, *Thames and Hudson, London, 1993*

IRELAND

The Living Legend of St Patrick, Alannah Hopkin, *Grafton Books, London, 1989*

MEXICO

In the Magic Land of Peyote, Fernando Benitez, *University of Texas Press, Austin, 1975*

Indian Running, Peter Nabokov, *Capra Press, Santa Barbara, 1981*

Rarámuri Souls, William M. Merrill, *Smithsonian Institution, Washington, 1988*

The Tarahumara, Wendell C. Bennett and Robert M. Zing, *The Rio Grande Press, Glorieta, New Mexico, 1976*

The Tarahumara of Mexico, Campbell W. Pennington, *University of Utah Press, 1974*

Tarahumara of the Sierra Madre, John G. Kennedy, *AHM Publishing, Illinois, 1978*

MYANMAR

Burma, Caroline Courtauld, *Odyssey Publications, Hong Kong, 1999*

The Burman, His Life and Notions, Sir George Scott, *Macmillan and Sons, London, 1910*

Burma As It Was, As It Is and As It Will Be, Sir George Scott, *George Redway, London, 1886*

POLAND

Misteria, Adam Bujak, *Wydawnictwo Warsaw, 1989*

RUSSIA

The Reindeer People, Marie Herbert, *Hodder and Stoughton, London, 1976*

SPAIN

A Guide to Andalucia, Michael Jacobs, *Viking, London, 1990*

España Oculta, Cristina García Rodero, *Lunwerg Editores, Madrid, 1989*

THAILAND

Thai Festivals, W. Warren and L. Invernizzi Tettoni, *Asia Books, Bangkok, 1989*

Thailand – Into the Spirit World, Marlane Guelden, *Asia Books, Bangkok, 1993*

TIBET

Touching Tibet, Niema Ash, *TravellersEye, Bridgnorth, Shropshire, UK 1999*

VIETNAM

Traditional Festivals in Vietnam, Do Phuong Quynh, *The Gyoi Publishers, Hanoi, 1995*

# index

Figures in italics indicate captions.

# To my wife Ingrid, who has been the most wonderful travelling companion

First published by MQ Publications Limited
12 The Ivories / 6–8 Northampton Street / London / N1 2HY
Tel: 020 7359 2244 / Fax: 020 7359 1616 / email: mail@mqpublications.com

Copyright © MQ Publications Limited 2002
Text copyright © Jeremy Hunter 2002

Design by Balley Design Associates

ISBN: 1 84072 283 5

Printed in the United Kingdom by Butler & Tanner
1 3 5 7 9 0 8 6 4 2

## photographer's notes

This project has taken over twenty-five years to complete – and there are still many festivals and celebrations I haven't been able to reach yet. The question I'm most frequently asked is not: 'Where was that taken?' but 'What camera did you use?'. It's as if the piece of equipment is more important than the creation of the image. Photographic equipment has radically changed over the past quarter of a century. Autofocus is now the norm and films have become sharper, faster and more colour saturated. I always say that my style of photography is principally about light, being in the right position, and squeezing the shutter at the appropriate moment. But how I achieved some of these photographs may be of interest:

**India/Kumbh Mela:** Canon EOS 1N/70–210mm Ultrasonic lens. Fuji film. Dhruv Singh, an Indian photographer based in Delhi, whom I met at the Kumbh, made all the difference here. He had fantastic contacts, and despite the fact that I had been unable to obtain a special Media Pass, which would have given me a priority status anywhere at the mela, he manoeuvred me into the perfect position, right in the middle of the Ganges as the nagas careened into the water.

**Tibet/Grand Summons:** I used a Voigtlander Bessa-R mostly here, with the 25mm f4 Skopar lens. I really like this camera. It's very light, the lenses are extremely sharp, virtually wholly manual, and extremely reliable in the very cold conditions which went as low as –20°C. SLR cameras rely heavily on batteries, which quickly discharge themselves in cold weather. That can be a problem at the crucial moment!

**Vietnam/Huong Tich:** Canon EOS 1N and Fuji Provia film.

**India/Ganguar:** Hassleblad X-Pan Panoramic camera.

**Russia/Praznik Cevera:** It reached –45°C here and that's a temperature that causes film to become very brittle and snap. Most of the sprocket holes ripped as a result. I used a Nikon-F.

**Malaysia/Goddess Amman:** Mostly shot with a Canon EOS 1N and 20-35 Ultrasonic zoom. Fuji Provia film really provided the richness and saturation of colour that this reportage required.

**India/Kartika Purnima:** Mamiya 6 x 7 and Fuji Velvia (50 ASA) film. I like to use medium format when I've the time, and there was an opportunity here.

**Bali/Galungan:** Canon EOS 1N with Fuji Provia 100 and 400 ASA film.

**Spain/El Pilar:** The important ceremonies here took place at night with the pilgrims lit mostly by candle light. I used Canon's technically superb (but heavy) 100–400mm image stabiliser lens which opens up new creative opportunities for shooting hand-held at slow speeds in very low light levels. Fuji Provia 400 ASA film.

All the other black and white photographs were taken on a Leica M6, mostly with the superb 21mm f2.8 Elmarit lens. Kodak T-Max or Ilford HP5 film throughout.

## acknowledgements

My thanks to Arvind Singh Mewar, HH Maharana of Udaipur, for his hospitality at the Pushkar and Ganguar festivals in India; Sabina Bailey in Udaipur and Satyajit Desai in Mumbai; Richard Bedser, Lizzie Bloom, Matt Dickinson, Noel and Louise Dockstader and Todd Osborne, who were all members of the *On the Horizon* television series with whom I made several wonderful festival journeys; Malcolm Beskin and Graham Westmoreland who first saw the material in this book and helped me in the early editorial stages; Patrick Brannelly at Emirates Airlines, Dubai; Steed Chan in Lanzhou, China, with whom I made two trips to Xiahe, Tibet; Les Chemins du Mont-Saint-Michel in Vire for inviting me to join them on their walk; Elisa Lopez in Lisbon for her assistance with the Portuguese festivals; Krystina Lyon-Budden; William L. Merrill at the Smithsonian Institution in Washington DC, who is a world authority on the Tarahumara in Mexico; Peter Oliver for translations of documents; Elizabeth Pytlarz in Cracow, Poland; and the Delhi-based photographer Dhruv Singh for 'navigating' us around the vast Kumbh Mela site in Allahabad.

I would also like to express my thanks to my editor Caroline Ball for her invaluable guidance in helping turn my scribbled notes into readable and, I hope, informative text; and finally to Zaro Weil and Ljiljana Baird at MQ who have been as passionate about *Sacred Festivals* as I have been for the past twenty-five years.